ENDORSEMENTS FOR *FRESH IDEAS FOR WOMEN'S MINISTRY*

Diana Davis knows women's ministry. It was my pleasure to watch her completely reinvigorate the ministry with women at First Baptist Church, Garland, Texas, where I served as an associate to Steve, her pastor husband. Diana is a pioneer. Her ideas are not only fresh, they work!

—David Francis
Director, Sunday School, LifeWay Church Resources
Nashville, Tennessee

Diana Davis is a woman who brings the love of Christ into everything she does. You will love her fresh bouquet of ideas that will spruce up your women's ministry.

—Jaye Martin
Women's Evangelism Strategist, NAMB, Atlanta, Georgia
Director of Women's Programs, Southern Baptist Theological Seminary
Louisville, Kentucky

Reading this book is an experience that engaged my emotions, my mind, and my inner being. I laughed, cried, took notes, and made plans of how to get this book into the hands of every Southern Baptist woman leader in Ohio because serving Jesus is at the heart of this design for women's ministry. The practical ideas, predesigned forms/checklists, and the priceless testimonies that saturate this work may be the answer to your prayers for God to work through both your Women On Mission and women's ministry groups.

—Cathy Pound
Women's Missions and Ministries Resource Group Leader
State Convention of Baptists in Ohio

Fresh Ideas for Women's Ministry offers a fresh look at starting, revitalizing, or supercharging today's women's ministries. Written by one who has done it, Diana Davis offers a wealth of strategies and plans from which any size church or ministry can benefit.

—Dr. Terri Stovall
Dean of Women's Programs; Associate Professor of Women's Ministries
Southwestern Baptist Theological Seminary
Fort Worth, Texas

I love this book. I have read several resources for women's ministry, yet *Fresh Ideas for Women's Ministry* has the most complete models for women's ministries I've ever seen. Diana's personal experiences shed insight for any church to develop a model that will succeed in a variety of settings as well as encourage missions and ministry.

—Cindy Goodwin
Director of Women's Missions and Ministries
Florida Baptist Convention

Whether a church wants to begin a women's ministry or fine-tune an existing one, *Fresh Ideas for Women's Ministry* has the answers. Every church needs a copy in its resource library. It works!

—Diane Fitzgerald
Women's Coordinator, First Baptist Church
Griffith, Indiana

Diana Davis is a wellspring of marvelous insights in ministering to women and *Fresh Ideas for Women's Ministry* is evidence of that. This book will provide women's ministry leaders great help in shaping a ministry of quality and purpose. Read it and get excited about the possibilities.

—Dr. Jim Witt
Associate Pastor, Missions and Assimilations, First Baptist Church
Garland, Texas

Diana's book with its "Get up and go!" attitude has a destination. That destination is actually to do what has been studied and planned. She invites us to join her in the celebration of the doing of God's word.

—Patty Hankins
Wife of Louisiana Baptist Executive Director

Diana's book not only offers fresh ideas that are practical and easy to implement, they are specific in getting women involved in the mission of God to reach the world beginning with their Jerusalem.

—Jaye Copeland
Childhood and WMU/Women's Ministry
State Convention of Baptists in Indiana

LIGHT is one of the best programs I have seen and worked with for training women in the Bible and in ministry!

—Glad Martin
Women's Ministry Leadership Team, First Baptist Church
Garland, Texas

Women's ministry helps keep the focus off *me* and puts it on others, as Christ would have it.

—Karen Witherspoon
Women's ministry participant
Singapore

LIGHT reaches across the age barriers, uniting women of faith in ministry for blessing the participants as well as the ministries in which they participate. Whether dividing sugar or assisting a client with clothing selection, the touch of the Master's hand is felt by those in need.

—Susan Boyd
Director of Benevolence Ministry, First Baptist Church
Garland, Texas

This book is a treasure for any women's ministry leader. It allows an intimidating job to become organized, fun, and rewarding.

—Sharon Butler
Women's Ministry Planning Team
Blairsville, Georgia

As a leader in women's ministry, I often need new ideas to keep things exciting and interesting. *Fresh Ideas for Women's Ministry* does not disappoint. Diana Davis has packed this book with fun and practical suggestions that will breathe new life into your church's women's ministry programs. Make use of her vast experience to reach the women of your church and community.

—Kathy Howard, MRE
Minister of Adult Education and author
Midland, Texas

fresh ideas
for *Women's* ministry

fresh ideas

for Women's ministry

diana davis

B&H
PUBLISHING GROUP

Nashville, Tennessee

ISBN-13: 978-0-7394-9743-2

Published by B&H Publishing Group
Nashville, Tennessee

Acknowledgments

This book is dedicated to the dozens of godly women who served alongside me as coleaders in women's ministry at First Baptist Churches in Humble and Garland. My heart-felt love and appreciation to each of you.

Thanks to my #1 encourager—my husband, Steve—for believing this book should be written.

I'm indebted to my editor, Tom Walters, for his expertise, and to managing editor Kim Stanford, who weaves it all together so beautifully.

Special thanks to Dixie Scogin for her logo design, Randy Lind for his chorus, and Jaye Copeland for her encouragement and input.

To my beloved partners and sisters across Indiana: I love serving alongside you, and admire your commitment to share Jesus with women in our state.

And to every woman who participated in our church's women's programs—hundreds of you over the years—thank you for the part you played in this story. Eternity has been impacted because of you. Keep on shining!

Contents

Introduction   1

Chapter 1   In the Beginning   9

Chapter 2   Begin with the Pastor   15

Chapter 3   State Your Purpose   19

Chapter 4   Survey   21

Chapter 5   Visionary Leaders   27

Chapter 6   Annual Planning   41

Chapter 7   The Kickoff Event   53

Chapter 8   The Friendship Factor   63

Chapter 9   Ministry Teams   75

Chapter 10   Fellowship Classes   97

Chapter 11   Child Care   115

Chapter 12   Group Projects   119

Chapter 13   Special Events   123

Chapter 14   Publicize   135

Chapter 15   Evaluations   147

Chapter 16   Postlude   155

Appendix 1   Checklist for Women's Ministry Coordinator   159

Appendix 2   Checklist for Luncheon Coordinator   161

Appendix 3   Checklist for Hospitality Coordinator   163

Appendix 4   Checklist for Ministry Teams Coordinator   165

Appendix 5   Checklist for Fellowship Class Coordinator   167

Appendix 6   Checklist for Promotion Coordinator   169

Appendix 7   Did Women of the Bible LIGHT?   171

Resources   175

Introduction

So you're considering beginning or improving a women's ministry at your church? You've got the right book!

Whether yours is a megachurch or a minichurch, whether you want a weekly daytime program or a monthly event, whether you're an experienced women's ministry leader or a newcomer, you'll find oodles of fresh ideas that can be tweaked to fit the unique women at your church.

Women today are seeking something more. Forget the cookie-cutter "sit and soak" plan from the last decade. Women want to impact their family, their community, and their world for Christ. A vibrant women's program must be fast paced, well planned, purposeful, and top quality.

Within these pages you'll find hundreds of proven tips, checklists, and plans for a vibrant women's ministry. You'll find organizational charts, evaluation forms, and job descriptions. Special boxed notations are interspersed to assist small churches. And you'll enjoy the ongoing story of how the author helped begin effective women's ministry programs in two churches. Fifteen sequential chapters will discuss everything from getting started to year-end evaluations.

Women's ministry is not "one size fits all," so some ideas in this book will fit your group perfectly; others will not. You'll find that you can easily adjust many of the ideas to fit your women's group.

> If your church already has a vibrant women's ministry group,
>   you'll find suggestions to enhance your program.
> If your group just needs some improvement,
>   you'll find ideas to help bring it back alive.
> If you have no women's group in your church,
>   you may be inspired to begin one!

So grab a pencil and a highlighter and get started. When you read an idea that excites you, circle it. If it inspires another idea, jot it in the margin. As you read, you may think of just the perfect leader for a ministry team or a great idea for promotion. Keep writing. If you see a suggestion that won't apply to your church, scribble through it. Use the book for brainstorming, for inspiration, for instruction. Use it as a reference book. Adjust the forms and charts to fit your women's ministry. Add your church name and make it your own. By the time you finish your first reading, you'll already be formulating parameters for a vibrant women's ministry to fit your church. (Many forms from this book are provided in downloadable format at www.dianadavis.org.)

But here's the most important instruction: *Do it!* Don't just study about it or dabble in it or talk about it. Seek God's direction in beginning or improving the women's ministry at your church. You're about to embark on an exciting adventure.

The story begins . . .

Like hundreds of others across the nation, our church struggled with this issue. How can our church have a quality women's ministry? Oh, we already had pieces of a women's program: sporadic Bible studies, a small missions group, a monthly quilting guild, an event here or there.

But vibrant? Definitely not.

Well attended? Hardly!

Alive? Barely.

So when the leaders of those small groups approached me—the new pastor's wife, requesting that I try to reorganize and bring those struggling pieces together to reach more women, I hesitated.

To be honest, I dug my heels in deep and refused flatly. Months later, however, God was still tugging at my heart about the dilemma.

After lots of prayer and encouragement from my pastor/husband, I embarked on a study of successful women's programs in various churches across our state. I interviewed the leaders of ten quality, well-attended women's ministry groups, ranging from Bible study groups to missions organizations to event-oriented fellowship groups.

One recurring observation I heard from those leaders was this: women need friends. Christian friendship must be built into a successful women's program.

I was most surprised to find that all ten of those leaders answered one of my interview questions exactly the same. "If you were beginning all over again to create a quality women's ministry in your church, what one element would you change?" The answer came back loud and clear: "I would focus on ministry."

One women's ministry leader stated, "I can convince a hundred women to show up for a Bible class, but I can't get one of them to carry a bag of groceries to the needy people across the street." Another complained, "There's nothing to do with 'ministry' in our women's ministry. It's all about us!" Others gave examples of internal strife, self-centeredness, and failed attempts to redirect their inwardly focused ladies groups to care about a lost and dying world around them.

My initial thought was, *We could do better than that.*

Snapshot of a Vibrant Women's Ministry

LIGHT: A Model that Works!

Picture this:

Women of all ages are flooding into your church building, and the excitement is high. Your weekly women's ministry is about to begin. Why are they attending in droves? Three reasons: it's quality, it's purposeful, and it's fresh.

The ladies immediately disperse into several different classes. Some attend a Bible study, some study missions, and still others take craft classes. An hour later, all the groups come together for a brief coffee and fellowship. There's energy and laughter and chatter. And genuine Christian friendships are developing right before your eyes.

During the next hour the women divide into ministry teams, such as hospital, homebound, newcomer, and benevolence teams; and they go out into the local community doing ministry projects in Jesus' name.

All those ladies are back at the church an hour later, smiling and waving good-bye to their friends. Each woman knows that her morning was spent in a worthwhile way, and she'll be back next week—ready to enjoy Christian fellowship, attend a quality class, and make a difference once again in her community.

But, wait. There's more! There are quarterly ladies luncheons, group projects, and a quality child-care program.

This vibrant women's ministry began with just a handful of women, and it attracted oodles of women of all ages. We called it LIGHT, and it enhanced our church's impact on women's lives, its fellowship, and its reputation in the community.

Do you like what you see? Women's ministry can work in your megachurch or small church. As you design a women's ministry program to fit your church, you'll discover one important secret: women's ministry must involve *ministry*.

Visual—A Portrait of Light

LIGHT—
One Example that Works!

Ladies

Intentionally

Going,

Helping,

Touching

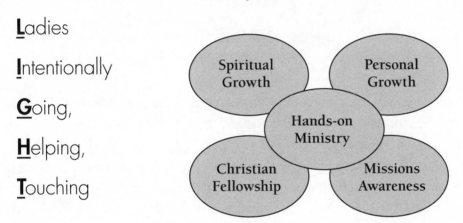

A Word from the Author

For the sake of illustration, I will share many examples in this book from a successful women's ministry at our church called LIGHT. No, I'm not suggesting that your women's ministry should look exactly like LIGHT. Your church's mission field is unique. Women at your church have different needs and distinctive qualities. As you begin to plan your women's ministry group, keep those distinctions in mind and formulate a women's ministry to fit your church. I *am* suggesting that you do *something!* I'm praying that in these pages you'll find many suggestions that can be applied to *your* church.

So what's the secret of LIGHT? It's in the name. The acronym LIGHT stands for **L**adies **I**ntentionally **G**oing, **H**elping, and **T**ouching. The emphasis of LIGHT is upward and outward.

The first hour of our weekly program provided an ever-changing variety of Bible, missions, and crafts classes. We called them "fellowship classes," and our overall attendance soared.

Yes, women study God's Word and apply it to their lives. We often offered several choices of Bible studies—some with homework, some without. Some topical, others expository. Life-changing Bible study is a vital part of any women's ministry.

And, yes, women study and support missions. In fact, our missions organization in both churches grew larger than it had ever been, and our church's missions education and support was exponentially enhanced. With our "upward and outward" purpose statement, missions are held high.

And, yes, we did offer crafts classes. I must admit that I wasn't sure that was a great idea at the beginning. Was it "holy" enough for our church women's group? But I quickly reneged on my hesitations. A ceramics or scrapbooking class often served as a hook for disinterested or periphery church members and unchurched attenders. Many of those found the joy of Christian friendship and ultimately met Jesus as their personal Savior.

But the biggest emphasis and heart of LIGHT was in that second hour of hands-on ministry teams. Carefully screened to fit Matthew 25:34–45, each team focused on ministering to the hurting, the needy, the sick, and the lonely. Ladies chose from several teams such as nursing home, welcome ministry, benevolence, and hospital teams. Team leaders carefully planned and prepared for that ministry to fit the allotted hour, and women left LIGHT in awe of how much they'd accomplished that morning!

The church was impacted. The community was impacted. The life of every participant was impacted. And eternity was impacted—all because we changed our women's ministry focus from ourselves to our God. From our own church friends to our lost world. From a "me" mentality to a "go ye" mentality.

Now before you begin to yawn, let me rush to tell you that women's ministry is fun! I've never heard more laughter in a church building than at women's ministry. Face it. It's fun to make new Christian friends. It's enjoyable to attend a well-prepared class for personal or spiritual growth. And it's joyful to shine for Jesus!

As you comb through this book, we'll discuss preplanning, planning, implementing, and evaluating your women's ministry as a sequential, cyclic process. You'll put in lots of hard work up front, but you'll be amazed at the results. The chapters enumerate twelve important elements to help you design a great women's ministry.

Are you ready to add some life to your women's ministry? No matter how God leads you to minister through the women in your church, perhaps some ideas in this book can be adapted to enhance your program. Take this story and make it your own. I'm praying that your women's ministry will shine brightly and LIGHT your part of the world!

The story, continues . . .

After my informal survey of several successful women's programs, I was encouraged. I began to pray for God's direction and wisdom. I began to listen more closely to women at the church, paying careful attention to needs and interests.

The more I listened, the more I learned. The more I learned, the more I became convicted. Suddenly every time I walked into the church, I'd observe a lonely woman. Just standing in a grocery line, I'd overhear women talking about a desire to make a difference. I'd drive by a nursing home or hospital and think, *We could go there!*

I realized how few women I really knew well, and I longed for a way to connect with other Christian women my age. And with older, wiser women. And with younger, growing women.

Then I realized that God had given me a great desire to help begin a women's ministry at our church.

CHAPTER 1

In the Beginning

I pursue as my goal the prize promised by God's
heavenly call in Christ Jesus.

—**Philippians 3:14**

My charming little Granny had the funniest sayings. In her high-pitched voice, she'd chirp, "You girls are like two peas in a pod," or, "Don't bite off more than you can chew." I can almost see her now, leaning out the back-porch door, hollering, "Hold your horses, honey!" She would draw out the word *hold* as if it had three syllables.

I'd be tearing out across the yard to go feed her chickens, and she'd say, "Hold your horses, honey. Grab the chicken feed first." Or I'd be racing out the door, and she'd say, "Hold your horses, Diana. You forgot your bag."

Sometimes, even today, I'll just get ahead of myself, jumping out ahead of the appropriate action. Oh, it's with the best of intentions. But jumping into deep water without thinking first can sometimes be disastrous, can't it?

You *know* there's a need for a quality women's ministry program at your church. You're sure that God has given you this desire for a good reason. And you're ready to jump in with both feet. But before you leap without looking, let me just say the words: *Hold your horses, honey!*

Now, all the good stuff is coming up in the next few chapters, all the planning and details and purposeful excitement. But first, take a look at your current situation. Visit with your pastor. Consider the goals of your women's ministry. The seemingly small details are strategic in setting the course ahead.

Where Are We?

WHAT?

❏ Bible study
❏ Missions support
❏ Ministry teams
❏ Ministry projects
❏ Fellowship group
❏ Luncheon/brunch
❏ Crafts group
❏ Events
❏ Other _____

WHO ATTENDS NOW?

❏ Mostly younger age
❏ Mostly older age
❏ Good age mix
❏ Church members
❏ Guests
❏ Unchurched

WHEN?

❏ Weekday a.m.
❏ Weekday p.m.
❏ Saturday a.m.
❏ Other _____

ATTENDANCE
PAST 6 MONTHS

Average #:   _____
Low #:   _____
High #:   _____
New #:   _____

Avg. church
attendance: _____

HOW OFTEN?

❏ Weekly
❏ Biweekly
❏ Monthly
❏ Occasionally

Where Are We?

It's just a fact. You need to know where you *are* before you can know where you're *going*. This chapter will help you with a self-analysis of your church's current women's program to determine a starting point.

You'll read three short stories about three different churches. The names have been changed to protect the innocent. (Kidding!) As you contemplate the stories, determine which most resembles your church.

SELECT A ONE-WORD DESCRIPTION

- ❑ Zilch: no women's ministries whatsoever
- ❑ Limited: needs attendance, purpose, or quality upgrade
- ❑ Dying: barely alive
- ❑ Self-centered: "sit and soak" mentality
- ❑ Scattered: might function better if groups united
- ❑ Vibrant: relevant and worthwhile, but ready to improve

ATMOSPHERE

- ❑ Joy
- ❑ Duty
- ❑ Purpose
- ❑ Intimidation
- ❑ Anticipation
- ❑ Boredom
- ❑ Excitement

OUR PASTOR THINKS WE'RE . . .

- ❑ Purposeful
- ❑ Enhancing the church
- ❑ Disconnected from church
- ❑ He doesn't know what we do
- ❑ He enthusiastically supports
- ❑ He hesitantly supports

OUR OVERALL FOCUS

- ❑ Inward focused (me)
- ❑ Outward focused (others)
- ❑ Focus on our God (Him)

I'd Give a Grade of

- ❑ A
- ❑ B
- ❑ C
- ❑ F

Example 1

Genesis Community Church has no iota of a women's ministry. They have a ladies' Sunday school class, but no weekday organization is planned specifically for women. No retreats or luncheons or weekday study groups. No occasional women's conferences or annual events.

Ginny is a longtime church member, but lately she's been thinking about a need she'd never noticed before. Wouldn't it be great to begin a women's ministry?

If this isn't your church, go directly to example 2. If it sounds familiar, keep reading.

If your church has no activities designed specifically for women, you're at the "Genesis" stage. If you, like Ginny, have been prompted by God to make a plan to reach women in your church and community, this book is for you. Every page will apply to your church! Go directly to page 14 and carefully, prayerfully read every word of this book.

Example 2

Bethel Baptist has several opportunities for women, but Becky observes that most women just ignore the announcements about them. There are a couple of sporadic Bible study groups and a small aerobics class. There's a missions group consisting of a few elderly saints. An annual mother-daughter banquet was once well attended but seems to have fizzled.

Becky loves her church, but she longs for regular Christian fellowship with other women. She's a busy young mother, but she would like to have a weekly program for women at her church where she would see women of all ages, grow as a Christian woman, and maybe even do something purposeful.

If this isn't your church, go directly to example 3. If it sounds familiar, keep reading.

Perhaps it's time to bring those disconcerted fragments of women's ministry together and begin afresh. By lovingly and prayerfully bringing existing groups together, their effectiveness may be enhanced. By unifying and adding benefit, individual groups may revive. You may decide to stop what you're doing and take a few weeks' break while you pray, plan, set goals, and start anew with a bang!

For example, when we began LIGHT, a previously existing Bible study group of middle-aged women was wary of changing their meeting day to join other groups. They finally agreed to give it a try. Their group grew immediately, and those ladies became involved in ministry teams, luncheons, and group projects. The change of meeting day had seemed overwhelming at first, but every member of the group was delighted with the results.

Another example: Two women in our church had visited homebound members for years, and they were ready for help. They expertly led the homebound ministry team to become one of our most effective groups. A missions group had dwindled to single-digit attendance, but by offering their quality program during the fellowship class hour, women of all ages joined them. Their group grew, and attendance exceeded the largest in their history.

Learning to "join hands" may be slightly uncomfortable at first. But the unity and multiplication is worth the effort.

Example 3

Women at Hope Bible Church love their women's ministry group. It's well attended, purposeful, and exciting. But, as wise leaders always do, Hannah and her leadership team are on the lookout for ways to improve their excellent program. Perhaps they need to upgrade promotional planning. Maybe they've become just a little self-centered and need to focus outward. Or maybe they're just looking for a few improvement tips for their group.

This is the book for you, Hannah. You and your team will probably enjoy the ideas more than all the others. Scour these pages. Ignore the parts you don't like and implement the ideas that fit Hope Church. There's always room for improvement.

Story time's over. Do any of these examples sound familiar? You've taken a realistic look at your current situation. Begin right now to pray and seek wisdom and discernment from God. If you feel that God is leading you to help begin or improve a women's ministry in your church, proceed to the next chapter.

What's Best?

Bible studies?   Fellowship?

Ministry teams?   Outreach events?

Missions?

Answer: Why not do it all?

CHAPTER 2

Begin with the Pastor

*Obey your leaders and submit to them, for they keep watch over your souls
as those who will give an account, so that they can do this with joy and
not with grief, for that would be unprofitable for you.*
—**Hebrews 13:17**

Women's ministry is exactly that, a ministry of your church. It is not a parachurch
organization or a church unto itself or a country club for the girls. Because it is a
ministry of your church, a right relationship between the pastor and the women's
ministry group is imperative.

Think about it: a necessary attribute of any leader is the ability to work under
proper authority. God has anointed your pastor as the leader of your church, so
if God has called you to help lead your church's women's ministry program, it is
essential that you joyfully line up under his leadership. God is not the author of
confusion. So before you gather a group of participants, before you tell everyone you
know about your plans, before you begin to set the direction and goal, visit with
your pastor.

Make an appointment to meet during the pastor's office hours. Avoid
Monday because most pastors are exhausted from Sunday's activities. When you

make the appointment, ask for half an hour of his time and state the purpose of your meeting: "I'd like to ask your opinion about the possibility of beginning a women's ministry program in our church." Drop a copy of this book by his office along with a brief note to confirm the appointment time.

Prepare for your meeting with the pastor as if everything depends on it. It does! Read everything you can find about women's ministry. Keep a notebook of ideas. Begin a folder for statistics about your church and community, success stories from other churches, and clippings that may apply to your circumstances.

Arrive exactly on time and arrive alone. Don't bring a gang of women friends. No husband sitting in the car or children holding your leg. Your attire should reflect the importance of the meeting. As always, modesty is critical for a Christian woman.

Summarize your initial thoughts about women's ministry in a few short sentences. Save your long orations and philosophizing for your husband or your dog. You can always expand your thoughts if he asks, but stay focused and succinct. Ask about your pastor's vision for women's ministry. Listen carefully and respectfully. Take notes. Be conscious of the time, and stick to your half-hour meeting appointment.

After you have shared your enthusiastic proposal, assure your pastor that you will only proceed if and when he endorses the plan. Then keep your word. Don't expect an instant answer. Your pastor may want to spend time in prayer and consideration of the proposal. He may need to present it to appropriate leaders or staff members. He may do further research or ask opinions from other pastor friends. Wait patiently for the answer. God's timing is perfect.

The story continues . . .

At both churches where we began a women's ministry, a one-year trial period was given. At the end of that year, the program would be evaluated and a determination made to continue or revert to the previous women's program. This accomplished two purposes: (1) it motivated our leaders to succeed; and (2) it allowed current groups to feel less intimidated by change.

After a year, there was absolutely no doubt. The success was enormous, and the church saw the fruit of the ministry.

If your pastor enthusiastically endorses the beginning of a women's ministry, discuss which member of the church staff or leadership team will be your liaison. Ask for his or her wisdom to determine a time line for leadership recruitment and unveiling the program. Allow a minimum of five months for a new women's ministry program's beginning. Additionally, a one-year trial period may be established.

If your pastor is less than enthusiastic, promptly withdraw your suggestion. Don't tell other church members about your disappointment. Do not say a negative word about the leader that God has called to serve in your church. Do not cross your arms or raise an eyebrow. And don't be disheartened and move to another church in order to get your way. Simply pray. The pastor may embrace the idea of women's ministry but have a different women's ministry leader in mind. Again, trust that God is in control, gracefully step aside, and truthfully pledge your support.

As a pastor's wife for decades, I have listened to other pastors bemoaning the headaches and tensions created by some women's groups. Be careful that women's ministry does not create an additional workload for your pastor. Your purpose is to help carry the ministry load. Determine now that your group will be a consistent asset to your church and a supporting arm of your pastor's and church's ministry. Enough said.

If your pastor and church express a desire to begin a women's ministry, it's time to get started!

CHAPTER 3

State Your Purpose

We make it our aim to be pleasing to Him.

—2 Corinthians 5:9

During the initial planning stages, take time to carefully prepare a purpose statement. All future decisions will be impacted by it. What should be the purpose of a women's ministry?

The focus of a country club is inward. Women's ministry is not a country club; however, participants' lives will be enhanced. The focus of a sorority group is fellowship and good deeds. Women's ministry is not a sorority, though we will definitely have fun and accomplish eternity-impacting good deeds. The purpose of a study group is learning. Women's ministry is much more than a study group, though we will learn and obey God's Word.

The purpose of a church women's ministry must focus upward and outward. James 1:22 challenges us to "be doers of the word and not hearers only." A church's women's group must have a purpose that is too big to fit into a select circle. It must not only feed and grow Christians but must accomplish the Great Commission as well.

Upward and Outward

A women's ministry must focus upward to glorify God. It should focus outward to impact the world for Him. Granted, the classes are designed for personal growth and spiritual growth, but a focal point of the program is the ministry teams, accomplishing hands-on ministry in Jesus' name.

It's what makes LIGHT *light*. It's what makes women's ministry *ministry*.

Display your purpose statement prominently at meetings. Print it on brochures and schedules. Type it at the bottom of posters and e-newsletters. Hold that target high.

Sample purpose statement: "To provide opportunities for women to know Jesus Christ, experience spiritual and personal growth, build Christian friendships, and share Jesus' love through hands-on ministry teams."

Without "Ministry" It's Just "Women's"

Remember I mentioned in the introduction that when I asked those ten women's ministry leaders the same question, "If you were beginning all over again to create a quality women's ministry in your church, what one element would you change?" Their answer was, "I would focus on ministry."

An upward and outward purpose statement, putting ministry at the heart of your program, can change the hearts of women in your church. It can change your women's ministry from a self-centered me-me-me mantra to an others-focused "go ye" purpose.

Shouldn't "women's ministry" have *ministry*?

CHAPTER 4

Survey

Now I am giving an opinion on this because it is profitable for you.
—2 Corinthians 8:10

How can you design the perfect women's ministry for your church or improve the effectiveness of your current group? Here's a novel answer: *ask them!*

A well-written survey can accomplish three significant purposes:

- *Create interest.* Excitement and discussions begin as each female member and guest receives the survey in the mail.

- *Help focus planning.* Your church is unique. A well-written survey will reveal needs, availability, and interests of the women in your church.

- *Discover potential leaders.* You'll find women in your church that may enjoy leading in women's ministry.

Design Your Survey

Using the sample survey (pages 23–24) as a starting point, carefully design a survey for the women of your church. Your goal is to get as many forms returned as possible, so the survey must be quick and easy to complete. This initial survey should fit on one side of one page of paper, leaving room on the back for handwritten comments. The survey should be well designed to reflect the quality of the upcoming women's ministry program.

Choices on the survey should reflect your purpose statement. Carefully word each question in a positive way, conveying enthusiasm and purpose. Ask about interests, child-care requirements, and dreams for a great women's program. To simplify responses, use check boxes. Ask only for name and phone or e-mail address. You can get more details later. Include a deadline date for survey submission.

Distribute the Survey

Allow three Sundays for the all-church women's survey. Begin on a Sunday and set the deadline date two Sundays later. Mail the survey to every female church member and recent visitor, timing its arrival just before the survey start date. Make plenty of extra copies and distribute surveys everywhere. Put them in church foyers, child-care areas, choir room, ladies' restroom counters, and Sunday school classes.

Send a personal note to women in leadership positions, such as church committee members, office workers, leaders of any current women's programs, department directors, and Sunday school teachers. Inform them about the survey, and ask for their input.

Collect the Surveys

Make it easy for ladies to submit their surveys. Put attractive collection boxes in visible locations around the church. Invite women to submit surveys in collection boxes, by mail, or online.

Print a brief announcement about the survey in church newsletters and bulletins, preparing distinct announcements for each Sunday. Use other forms of Sunday communication as appropriate at your church, such as Sunday school or pulpit announcements, church newsletter, Web site, or e-mail reminders.

Plaster church hallways, bulletin boards, and women's restrooms with visual reminders about the survey. Use a consistent color scheme or graphic, such as a giant question mark. Signs can read, "What do you think?" Set a goal to collect surveys from 80 percent of females at your church.

Women want and need fellowship and ministry opportunities. They're just waiting for your survey!

Wonder Woman in a Box

A unique display may attract attention. This one stopped traffic! A caped and modestly costumed Wonder Woman posed as a frozen mannequin inside a huge Plexiglas box. At first glance, the sign above the rigid form read "Wonder Woman," but the small print revealed the real message:

First Baptist wants a

Wonder ful **Woman**'s program.

Complete your survey today.

Women's Survey

Help our church create the perfect women's ministry.

If we could create the perfect women's ministry for our church, how would it look? Check all your preferences below and write comments and ideas on the back.

WHEN? The best time for me to be involved would be (check all possible times):

❑ **Weekday Morning**
Circle days: M T W TH F
❑ Weekly ❑ Biweekly
❑ 9:00 ❑ 9:30 ❑ 10:00
❑ 1 hour ❑ 2 hours ❑ 2½ hours

❑ **Weekday Evening**
Circle days: M T W TH F
❑ Weekly ❑ Biweekly
❑ 6:00 ❑ 7:00 ❑ 8:00
❑ 1 hour ❑ 2 hours

❑ **Saturday Morning**
❑ Biweekly ❑ Monthly
❑ 9:00 ❑ 9:30 ❑ 10:00
❑ 1 hour ❑ 2 hours

WHAT? The main focus of our perfect women's ministry would be:

❏ Ministry   Hands-on ministry teams to impact our town for Christ
❏ Bible Study   Life-changing Bible study classes
❏ Craft Classes   Personal growth and fellowship
❏ Missions Class   Exciting missions education and support
❏ Combination   More than one of those checked above

Please check all that might interest you below.

	I'm interested in Attending	Leading		I'm interested in Attending	Leading
Hospital team	❏	❏	Prison ministry team	❏	❏
Outreach team	❏	❏	Servant ministry team	❏	❏
New baby team	❏	❏	Shut-in ministry team	❏	❏
Food pantry team	❏	❏	Prison correspondence	❏	❏
New move-in team	❏	❏	Bible study	❏	❏
Love crafts team	❏	❏	Weight loss/Bible	❏	❏
Tape ministry team	❏	❏	Parenting class	❏	❏
Quill ministry team	❏	❏	Craft class	❏	❏
Clothes closet team	❏	❏	Women on Mission	❏	❏
Library outreach	❏	❏	Witnessing class	❏	❏
School mentor team	❏	❏	Book reviews	❏	❏
Nursing home team	❏	❏	Support group _____	❏	❏

Extra elements I'd enjoy:

❏ Missionary support projects   ❏ Mentoring younger women
❏ Christian friends   ❏ Ladies luncheons
❏ Prayer partners   ❏ Annual ladies retreat

Ages of my children requiring child care _____

If our women's program was top quality and meaningful, I'd probably attend:
❏ Regularly   ❏ Occasionally   ❏ Rarely

Name _____ Phone/E-mail _____

Please add other ideas on reverse side. Thanks for your input.

Do Something with Survey Results: An Informational Tea

Once you've collected the surveys, carefully and quickly compile the results. Meet again with the pastor or staff liaison for wisdom and direction, and then schedule an informational tea with those who indicated an interest in leadership. The purpose of the tea is to generate excitement, grant information, and recruit leadership.

Schedule the tea at the approximate time of day that you hope your women's group will meet. For example, if you are considering a Tuesday morning group, plan the tea for Tuesday. The tea can be at your home, a tea shop, or a nice room at the church.

Make personal contact with each woman who indicated an interest in leadership, giving her two weeks' notice before the tea. An e-mail invitation is not appropriate; a formal invitation is not necessary. Follow up with a reminder note or e-mail, restating the date, location, and beginning and ending time for the tea. Ask each potential leader to pray for the upcoming women's ministry.

Provide competent child care during the tea, and ask mothers to make a reservation so appropriate workers can be provided. If possible, add a special treat of some kind for the children.

Design a leadership interest survey (sample on page 26), listing possible opportunities for leadership in women's ministry such as officer positions, ministry teams, classes, and minor responsibilities. Prepare a fifteen-minute presentation to overview plans for women's ministry and opportunities for leadership. Prayerfully rehearse how you will cast a vision for women who attend.

Although the tea will be informal and relaxed, plan it well. Set a vase of fresh flowers on an entry table, play background music, and provide a sign-in sheet and name tags. Simple refreshments should be beautifully presented.

As they arrive, serve snacks and encourage informal fellowship. After about fifteen minutes, invite ladies to be seated for the brief program. If the pastor's wife is able to attend, ask her ahead of time if she will lead an opening prayer. Emphasize that these are the beginning stages of an exciting endeavor and that no assignments or decisions will be made today. Use visuals or audiovisuals to enthusiastically present a basic overview of potential plans, time lines, and leadership needs.

After the presentation, ask ladies to divide into groups of three and pray for God's blessings and wisdom. After a few minutes dismiss by reading a Scripture and offering a prayer of praise and thanksgiving to God.

Ask ladies to complete a leadership interest form. Emphasize that the form is not an obligation but simply an indication of their interest. Assure the women that you will contact them soon about their participation. Collect the leadership forms as they leave.

Leadership Interest Survey

NAME _____

PHONE/E-MAIL _____

Please check all possible areas of interest, circling your first choice.

❏ Coordinate ministry teams
❏ Coordinate publicity
❏ Coordinate fellowship classes

❏ Coordinate registration
❏ Coordinate outreach luncheons
❏ Coordinate hospitality

Lead a ministry team. (List teams needing leader.)

❏ Welcome wagon
❏ Homebound

❏ Nursing home
❏ Prison

❏ Outreach
❏ Other _____

Lead a class (6 to 12 weeks).

❏ Craft class _____
❏ Bible class _____

❏ Missions group
❏ Special interest class _____

Weekly

❏ Greeter
❏ Lead special project
❏ Office assistance
❏ Help with _____

❏ Snack coordinator
❏ Computer assistance
❏ Special event planning

Quarterly outreach luncheon

❏ Coordinate luncheon table hostesses
❏ Luncheon setup and cleanup

❏ Luncheon decor
❏ Luncheon table hostess

CHAPTER 5

Visionary Leaders

When the leaders lead . . . , when the people volunteer, praise the LORD.
—Judges 5:2

Take a look at successful women's ministry programs, and you'll find a common element: effective leadership. God calls out a visionary leader, pairs her with a committed leadership team, and great things happen.

The Leadership Team

A worthwhile women's ministry will involve many women in various areas of leadership from greeters to class leaders to luncheon planners. A small group of officers, composed of the coordinator of each major area of the women's ministry program, forms the leadership team.

These leaders of leaders will spend many collective and individual hours of administrative planning for your women's ministry. They'll meet together weekly for prayer before the women's ministry. In our model women's ministry, the leadership team consists of the following officers:

Officers/Leadership Team Members

Women's ministry coordinator—provides overall leadership for
 women's ministry
Ministry teams coordinator—recruits and oversees ministry teams
Fellowship class coordinator—recruits and oversees classes
Luncheon/event coordinator—oversees luncheon team
Hospitality coordinator—coordinates registration, greeters, snacks
Publicity coordinator—oversees promotion
Pastor's wife—ex-officio member for wisdom and encouragement

The concept of a leadership team will positively impact your entire women's ministry. With each officer working to accomplish her task, and at the same time working as a part of the overall women's ministry picture, much is accomplished! Rather than being a one-woman show or a hit-and-miss annual cycle of officers, a leadership team provides a continuity of leadership and a diversity of ideas and age range.

In our model women's ministry, a leadership team of six women works together for annual planning and weekly ministry oversight. The women's ministry coordinator is the leader, and each member of the leadership team is responsible for a specific area of the women's ministry program. This leadership team of officers also leads in planning group projects and kickoff events.

Women's Ministry Leadership Team

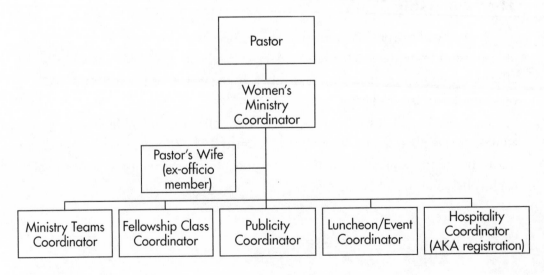

Each member of the leadership team is an active, supportive member of the church. She realizes that other women are observing her lifestyle and priorities, and attempts to model a godly lifestyle. She works in harmony with the rest of the leadership team, arriving early to ascertain that her part of the ministry runs smoothly each week. Leadership team members need good administrative skills, superb people skills, and a strong commitment to God and the church.

Most important, she must be a woman of respect. If I asked you to write the name of the church gossip or troublemaker in the left margin, you would know exactly whose name to write. (Don't write it! This is just an illustration.) *She* is not a potential officer. She can help in dozens of other small ways, but to place her in leadership would set an unhealthy precedent. The selection of godly, committed leaders is absolutely critical to the success of a women's ministry. Notice that I didn't say perfect princesses. All are sinners, we know, but choose women of good reputation as leaders.

Expectations for All Women's Ministry Leaders

__ A Christian, a committed member of our church
__ Growing relationship with God
__ Faithful preparation for duties
__ Faithful attendance and early arrival at weekly women's ministry
__ Joyful collaboration with leaders
__ Minimum of one-year commitment (officers and ministry teams)

If the pastor's wife is willing, invite her to serve as an ex-officio member of the leadership team to offer wisdom and encouragement. If she has a desire to serve in another leadership position, praise God! In our church the current president of our Women on Mission group also served on our leadership team. This was extremely beneficial to help with our missions focus.

Use the sample job descriptions to create parameters for your women's ministry officers. A longer checklist for each officer's responsibilities is found in the appendix.

Women's Ministry Coordinator

Job Description

- Oversees and gives direction to the entire women's ministry program
- Recruits leadership team members
- Schedules and leads marathon planning meeting and officers' meetings
- Assists officers with resources, training, and encouragement
- Serves as the liaison to the church staff
- Gives oversight to fall and spring kickoff events
- Officiates at weekly coffee, quarterly luncheons, and kickoff events
- Gives direction and oversight to group projects

Ministry Team Coordinator*

Job Description

- Oversees and gives direction to ministry teams
- Determines a variety of relevant hands-on ministry teams
- Interviews and recruits a leader for each ministry team
- Provides detailed ministry team information to promotion coordinator
- Helps equip, train, and encourage ministry team leaders
- Regularly reports statistics of ministry team contacts
- Keeps a notebook of potential leaders and ministry teams
- Plans an annual social gathering for ministry team leaders
- Attends marathon planning meeting and leadership team meetings

*First officer position recruited after women's ministry coordinator

Fellowship Class Coordinator

Job Description

- Oversees and gives direction to fellowship class hour
- Plans schedule of Bible, missions, and personal growth classes, adding new classes each semester
- Identifies, interviews, and recruits a qualified leader for each class
- Approves Bible study curriculum with church staff
- Provides detailed class information to promotion coordinator
- Encourages and assists fellowship class leaders
- Keeps a notebook of potential classes and teachers
- Provides a social gathering for fellowship class leaders each semester
- Attends marathon planning meeting and leadership team meetings

Hospitality Coordinator

Job Description

- Oversees registration, greeters, and coffee break
- Recruits assistants for greeting, registering, and coffee break setup
- Gives oversight to directory, name tags, budgeting, fellowship needs
- Provides attendance reports to church office along with guest data
- Prepares a one-page annual report
- Attends marathon planning meeting and leadership team meetings

Luncheon Coordinator*

Job Description

- Oversees and gives direction to four quarterly outreach luncheons
- Recruits a team for luncheon planning
- Procures an approved speaker for luncheons
- Provides luncheon details to promotion coordinator
- Keeps an organizational notebook for future luncheon coordinator
- Attends marathon planning meeting and leadership team meetings

*One-year responsibility.

Publicity Coordinator

Job Description

- Oversees and gives direction to publicity for women's ministry program, both inside and outside the church
- Plans one-year promotion calendar
- Collects information from officers to design women's ministry brochure
- Recruits assistants to implement promotion items
- Keeps a notebook of publicity resources
- Attends marathon planning meeting and leadership team meetings

How to Find Leaders

This book is written on the premise that God has called a woman to coordinate your church's women's ministry. If your church has a paid women's ministry staff position, she would naturally serve in the leadership role. If the position is volunteer (as in many churches of all sizes), this leader must be enthusiastically endorsed by the church's pastor and leaders. If you are reading this book, it is possible that God has given you a desire to begin or improve a women's ministry in your church.

As the women's ministry coordinator prayerfully considers potential leadership team members, she studies responses from the all-church survey, the interest forms from the introductory coffee, and year-end evaluation forms. She may ask for input from church staff or leaders for additional names. She will study the job descriptions and consider each woman's qualifications and skills, carefully including women of every age group in the leadership team. This is an important step, and she should ask for God's wisdom as she prepares a list of potential officers.

When a women's ministry coordinator begins to build her leadership team, she should avoid the temptation to recruit her personal friends as officers. There will be many opportunities for each of them to serve in some way. Leaders should come from a variety of groups within the church. Additionally, she must not settle for mediocre leaders. Quality, godly leadership will produce a quality, godly women's ministry.

In the model women's ministry, many amazing, quality, previously untapped leaders surfaced—working women with flexible schedules, new church members with great enthusiasm, a recently retired schoolteacher, a stay-at-home mom with executive-level skills. Even though many of your leaders will hold current leadership positions, don't limit leadership responsibilities to women who have held previous leadership positions within your church. It is imperative that new women are included as leaders.

After meeting with the pastor or staff liaison for their input, the women's ministry coordinator will make an initial contact with potential officers.

Your leadership team members are sitting in your church pews, waiting for a challenge to serve their God. Find them.

The story continues . . .

We were planning a fashion-show method of introducing LIGHT leaders at one year's kickoff when I made a surprising discovery. Every single one of our leadership team, fellowship class leaders, and ministry team leaders were actively involved as leaders in our church's Sunday school. They were Sunday school teachers in adult, youth, children, or preschool classes. Some were department directors, Sunday school greeters, and class outreach leaders.

Oh, I suppose that shouldn't have been such a shock, but it made a great script for our emcee as they walked the runway in their boutique outfits. The "fashion description" words said nothing about the gorgeous clothing they modeled. Instead, it described each woman's involvement in our local church, beginning with her Sunday school involvement, and then told about the officer position, or the ministry team, or the class she would lead.

That discovery taught me something. It's true that many previously untapped leaders were discovered who contributed to the leadership and effectiveness of LIGHT over the years. But often those women who have a heart for sharing the good news of Christ are vitally involved in the Bible study ministry of your church already. They know the excitement of serving Him and may joyfully accept an additional challenge.

How to Recruit Leaders

The women's ministry coordinator will personally recruit each member of the leadership team, meeting individually with each potential officer. Because ministry is a priority, she will recruit the ministry team coordinator first, then the other team members.

Call the potential leader and give a brief overview of your request. If she is interested, make an appointment to meet together. Ask her to share her Christian testimony and how God is working in her life.

Give her an overview of the women's ministry plan, and explain her potential ministry position. Let her know that the pastor has recommended her. Give her a printed copy of the proposed job description and share your vision for her area of ministry. Discuss how you feel her skills and gifts will fit the job.

If she indicates an interest, ask her to pray about accepting this responsibility. Encourage her to call you if she needs further clarification, and request that she get back with you about her decision. Pray together, asking God's blessings on the new women's ministry and His direction for its leadership. Call her in a few days to ask about her thoughts.

If she responds positively, praise God! Refer her to resources that may help with her new responsibility, and invite her for an informal gathering for the leadership team. Give her the date for the marathon planning meeting.

Should you take no for an answer? Absolutely! Never forget that our mighty God is in control, and it's not your job to coerce women to serve Him. The woman who declines a position may prefer to be a participant instead of a leader or may enjoy a different responsibility. Trust God to direct her decision.

Before the initial marathon planning meeting, leadership team members should meet informally as a group. Plan coffee in your living room, and invite each leader to share her personal testimony with the others. Chat about dreams and ideas for the upcoming women's ministry. Share ideas with one another about women who might assist in various areas. Talk about family. Offer encouragement. Help them to get to know one another.

From this point each officer will take over her area of ministry, consulting regularly with the women's ministry coordinator. She will begin immediately to recruit assistants needed to complete her assigned tasks.

After the first year of women's ministry, the standing officers are invited to remain in their position. The exception is the luncheon coordinator, which is a one-year responsibility. To fill vacated leadership team positions, a special meeting is planned for a nominating team composed of the current officers and the senior pastor's wife. End-of-year evaluation forms may reveal potential leaders, and the outgoing officer may also have suggestions for her successor. The women's ministry coordinator contacts the potential new officer for her acceptance, and then the new slate of officers is introduced at the final luncheon.

Small Church Tip

In a small church almost every participant may have a responsibility when you first begin a women's ministry. As new women attend, share the workload. Job descriptions may be combined easily. Assign responsibilities by women's gifts and interests.

Train Leaders

Encourage leaders to become an expert in their ministry area. They can read books, gather printed materials, study Internet resources, and chat with women in similar ministries. Watch for training opportunities such as your denomination's associational, state, and national training events. The missions organization has a wonderful resource in the Woman's Missionary Union, who provides excellent training and materials. Many denominations offer online chat groups in various ministry areas as well.

Officers may also meet monthly or as needed. Our officers often met biweekly or monthly. Sometimes we met early on LIGHT day or afterward for lunch. The actual meeting rarely lasted more than half an hour, with each member of the leadership team presenting a brief, often printed, report about her area of ministry. We used an agenda similar to the one below.

Leadership Team Monthly Meeting
Agenda

8:00 a.m.	Promotion Update	Promotion Coordinator
8:05 a.m.	Attendance Report	Hospitality Coordinator
8:10 a.m.	Fellowship Class Report	Fellowship Class Coordinator
8:15 a.m.	Ministry Teams Report	Ministry Team Coordinator
8:20 a.m.	Luncheon Report	Luncheon Coordinator
8:25 a.m.	Update and Prayer	Women's Ministry Coordinator
8:30 a.m.	Dismiss	Women's Ministry Coordinator

Additional Leaders

Each member of the leadership team will recruit and train her own team of women to assist with her task, working both independently and in harmony with the whole. For example, the ministry team coordinator will prayerfully determine needed ministry teams and, after approving them through proper channels, will recruit a leader for each ministry team, such as hospital, welcome wagon, and nursing home. She assists those ministry team leaders with resources, training, and encouragement.

In our LIGHT women's ministry model, the ministry team coordinator was given a two-week head start to recruit ministry team leaders first. For example, our leadership team met for an initial brainstorming meeting, and everyone there shared ideas for women who might enjoy serving in various areas. After that meeting the ministry team coordinator was given a couple of weeks to begin recruiting her ministry team leaders, and then the rest of the officers gathered their assistants. A list of possible assistants for each officer follows:

- *Ministry team coordinator.* Her team consists of the leader of each ministry team, such as hospital, welcome wagon, etc. In consultation with the women's ministry coordinator and church staff liaison, she prayerfully determines which ministry teams will be offered, and discovers a leader for each. (See page 30 for the job description.)

- *Fellowship class coordinator.* Her team consists of one teacher for each of the classes offered during the fellowship class hour. (See page 31 for job description.)

- *Hospitality coordinator.* She recruits greeters and registration table assistants. She is also responsible for bookkeeping, weekly and annual reports, coffee break preparation, and historical scrapbooking and may recruit assistants for those jobs. (See page 31 for the job description.)

- *Luncheon coordinator.* She recruits a team of women to plan the quarterly luncheons, involving women with decor, food, tickets, hostesses, etc. (See page 32 for the job description.)

- *Publicity coordinator.* She recruits a team of women gifted in graphic arts, marketing, computer technology, and design. The church secretary may be a part of this team. (See page 32 for the job description.)

The sample organizational chart for a small church, below, begins with three officers with multiple responsibilities. As new women become involved, they relinquish some of their leadership responsibilities to other women.

Small Church Organizational Chart

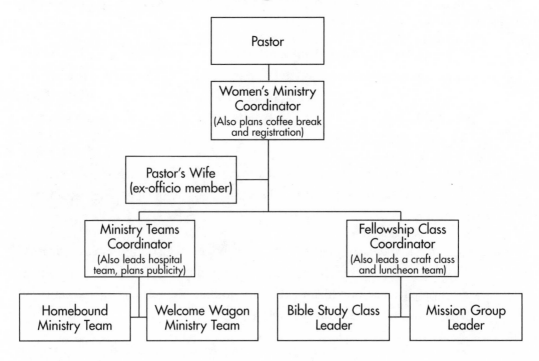

The second sample organizational chart is from one semester of our model women's ministry.

Sample Women's Ministry Organizational Chart

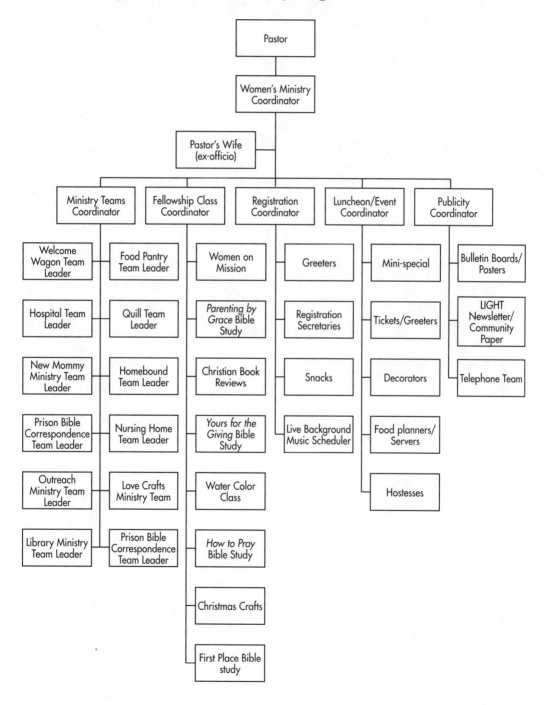

The story continues . . .

Ann was a beautiful young mother, a pediatric nurse at our local hospital, and a committed Christian.

On the women's ministry survey form, she checked lots of boxes to indicate her interest in beginning a women's ministry at our church. At the bottom she wrote these words, "I'll help with anything, but I'm not a leader." She came to the coffee for potential leaders, with the comment, "Just don't ask me to lead anything!"

As our kickoff date approached, we still had no one to plan the luncheons. Ann called just before our deadline and said, "I'm still not a leader, but I think God wants me to organize the luncheons."

Because God was the recruiter, He provided the ability. Ann was the best organizer I've ever seen! Those luncheons were done "as unto the Lord" and with a humble spirit and willing hands. They became a key to reaching many women for Christ that year. Ann later stepped into a leadership role with ministry teams, and she was a natural as she encouraged and delegated and organized.

It's been many years since she decided to take that leadership role. Ann (the "I'm not a leader" Ann) is now head of nursing at the hospital, leading dozens of women on a daily basis. She's still vitally involved in the church's women's program, and she testifies, "If I had not taken that role, I would never have developed the confidence and skills I need to do this job today."

Add Music

Look for ways to add music to enhance the atmosphere at women's ministry.

- Play recorded background Christian music everywhere it's appropriate.
  —In the registration area
  —During the knitting class
  —While the quill ministry writes notes
  —During coffee fellowship and mealtime of luncheon

- Provide live piano music as women arrive at a luncheon or event.

- For a large group, make a rotation list for pianists to play background music during the coffee break.

- Sing a short theme chorus in unison at the end of coffee break (see sample on page 74).

CHAPTER 6

Annual Planning

Plans fail when there is no counsel,
but with many advisers they succeed.
                                                    —Proverbs 15:22

Well before the first meeting day, careful planning must occur. Planning takes time on the front end, but good planning will result in a quality, worthwhile program.

In this chapter we'll discuss how to plan a day, a semester, and a year's schedule. A marathon planning meeting will be used as an annual planning tool with officers. Plan well. It's worth your effort.

Quote from Survey

"Our church's LIGHT women's ministry is the brightest spot in my very busy schedule."

The perfect women's ministry schedule for my church will be different from yours. No day of the week or time of the day will fit every woman who wants to attend, but careful consideration about your meeting time will enhance attendance.

Morning, Evening, or Weekend?

Would full-time working women attend an evening women's ministry? Would stay-at-home moms, retirees, and flex-hour workers enjoy a morning ministry time? To schedule your women's ministry at an optimum time, carefully tally responses from your all-church survey to determine if more women would attend morning or evening weekdays, or Saturday. A great women's ministry must have great leaders, so give special attention to responses of potential leaders.

Day of the Week?

Our survey results showed that most women interested in a daytime meeting could attend on Tuesday or Thursday. Since our church's Mothers Day Out met on Thursdays, we selected Tuesday mornings for our meeting day. When selecting a day of the week, consider your church's calendar, survey statistics, and community and school holidays and schedules. For example, Mondays and Fridays may not be desirable because of three-day weekends. Wednesday may be difficult if your church has a midweek service.

The story continues . . .

Our church was in a town where most women worked outside the home, so we seriously considered an evening women's ministry program. However, our survey revealed that all potential leaders were stay-at-home moms, work-at-home women, and retirees who preferred a daytime program. We decided to begin our first year with a daytime ministry.

We were in for a shock. Women came from everywhere! We had no idea so many women of all ages were interested in a quality daytime women's ministry. The range of women was extreme—from college age to elderly, from professionals to mommies, from mature saints to brand-new Christians.

One segment of women that we hadn't considered were working women with flexible work schedules—nurses, realtors, saleswomen, part-time workers, etc. Because the plan was fast paced and worth their morning, working women made up as much as a third of our attendance.

After a year we added a monthly evening group, NightLIGHT. Its purpose was identical, but programming was prepared to fit a working woman's interests and schedule. A separate leadership team was formed, and LIGHT and NightLIGHT met together for an annual retreat.

Weekly, Biweekly, or Monthly?

Our initial planning team was discussing whether to meet weekly or biweekly. Mine was the only no vote when the group decided to meet weekly. I was fairly certain that a weekly meeting was overkill for today's women, but, boy, was I wrong! A weekly daytime meeting gives continuity, simplifies promotion, and provides greater impact in ministry and fellowship.

An evening version of women's ministry may function well biweekly or monthly. Determine the schedule that best fits your church.

What Time?

Use your purpose statement to determine the needed amount of time a typical meeting will require. Keep in mind that women have busy schedules, so it should be a compact, worth-her-minutes schedule. It should have a relaxed feeling, but time should be carefully planned and purposeful.

Our plan included a time for me, a time for us, and a time for God. It would consist of a first hour of fellowship classes (for me), a second hour for ministry teams (for Him), and a fifteen-minute coffee break fellowship between (for us). Our weekly women's ministry, then, would require two hours and fifteen minutes.

Next, consult with your church staff liaison to choose a beginning and ending time for your meetings. Planning around preschoolers' naptime, church building availability, school hours, and mealtime can be tricky. We scheduled our weekly meeting from 9:30 a.m. to noon.

Model Women's Ministry Weekly Schedule

9:30 a.m.	Fellowship Classes	"For Me"
10:30 a.m.	Coffee Fellowship	"For Us"
10:45 a.m.	Ministry Teams	"For Him"
Noon	Child Care Closed	

Selecting a meeting time for an evening schedule is slightly more difficult. Consider mealtime, children's bedtime, and drive time from work. Our NightLIGHT group met on the second Thursday of each month from 6:30 to 8:00 p.m.

The story continues . . .

Our annual evaluation forms were submitted anonymously. No names were allowed. We did, however, request that women place a check mark by their age group. As I studied survey results from several consecutive years, one fact glared at me: younger women want a fast-paced women's program, and older women want a relaxed pace.

There are exceptions, of course, but year after year, ladies in younger age groups would comment, "Speed it up just a little," and women in older age groups would say, "Slow it down just a tad."

As you plan your women's ministry, keep that in mind. Cram every ounce of energy and excitement possible into every minute of your weekly program, but keep the overall atmosphere relaxed and casual.

Plan a Year

In our model program, annual planning was done at an intensive all-day marathon planning meeting, attended by all six leadership team members. The meeting took place in March, and planning was done for the upcoming fall and spring semesters. When women's ministry began in the fall, the entire year's printed schedule was unveiled and given to attenders.

Each semester's schedule offers some new classes and ministry team choices. Preplanning will increase attendance. For example, a woman who commits to teach a ceramics class next spring will most likely attend all year, and she will bring her friends. A woman who is intrigued with involvement in the nursing home ministry team will probably attend a class as well.

Sample Refrigerator Magnet Calendar

LIGHT 2010–2011 CALENDAR
First Baptist Church
Ladies Intentionally Going, Helping, Touching

LIGHT meets Thursdays, 9:30 a.m. to Noon for
classes and ministry teams.

SPECIAL EVENTS

August 17	Road Rally Kickoff Event
November 30	Christmas Workshop
December 7	Christmas Missions Program
January 11	House Slipper Tea Kickoff

LUNCHEONS*

October 5	Harvesting Happiness, Rosemary Almond
December 14	Sounds of the Season, Julie Parker
February 8	You Light Up My Life, Jen Johanson
May 3	Life's No Picnic, Penny Alexander

Fall Semester
Session 1: 8/24–9/28
Session 2: 10/12–11/16

Spring Semester
Session 3: 1/18–3/1
Session 4: 3/22–4/26

*No LIGHT on luncheon days, Thanksgiving,
Christmas break, or spring break.

Quote from Survey (woman in her thirties)

"When I interviewed for my job, I negotiated to have Thursday mornings off so I could continue attending LIGHT. It's *so* worth my morning!"

The Marathon Planning Meeting

The annual marathon planning meeting is a critical organizational day of brainstorming, scheduling, and enmeshing the various parts of the women's ministry program.

Plan the date for the marathon planning meeting well in advance, working with individual officers to ascertain when all can attend. Set aside five hours—a real marathon. For example, meet from 9:00 a.m. to 2:00 p.m. or 11:00 a.m. to 4:00 p.m. Alternately, the marathon could be done as a retreat. It's the one required meeting for your women's ministry leadership team. Leaders make arrangements for their children, shut off cell phones, close the door, and plan the entire year's calendar.

Various individuals may be scheduled to stop by at a designated time on the agenda for a report. For example, if your group plans to make a cookbook next fall, the person who will oversee the project may be scheduled to make a ten-minute presentation. The person who oversees child care could be scheduled to give a fifteen-minute presentation. The pastor may be available to stop by for the last few minutes of the meeting day to pray for leaders.

The women's ministry coordinator prepares and prints a meeting agenda with a specific discussion time assigned for each item. You have a lot to plan during this meeting, so a detailed agenda is necessary (sample on page 47).

In preparation for the meeting, the women's ministry coordinator has met with the pastor or church staff liaison for input and wisdom about the overall program. She has gathered materials, such as the church calendar, school calendar, community event dates, map, church directory, and telephone book. She has compiled results of the church survey and women's ministry evaluations and printed the results. She has ordered lunch to be delivered at a specified time, selecting a simple menu of finger foods. (You certainly don't get to stop planning just to eat!)

She arranges the meeting room so the officers are seated around a table. Agendas and reports are placed at each seat and perhaps a small gift for each officer. A few chairs are set to the side for those who will stop by to report. The purpose statement and theme Scripture are prominently displayed. It looks like an important meeting. It is an important meeting. During these hours most of the preparation for next year's ministry will be planned. Take it seriously.

The key elements of the meeting are calendar scheduling, brainstorming, and evaluating. Each officer presents a summary report about her area of ministry, using handouts or visuals. She carefully uses her allotted time to inform the other officers and takes advantage of the opportunity to solicit their input for improvements, ideas, and new leaders. Theme and leadership responsibilities will be planned for the kickoff event. Officers will set attendance goals and ministry goals, discuss problem areas, and plan next year's group projects.

Before you begin to think this is a torturous process, let me inject this thought: this was the most fun meeting of the year! Yes, we worked hard. But we also laughed, shared, prayed, and enjoyed one another.

Small Church Tip

Just because your church is small doesn't mean you don't plan! Planning is equally important in a small church. Almost every detail of this chapter will apply to your church.

Sample Agenda

Marathon Planning Meeting

Thursday, March 12, Noon to 5:00 p.m.

Noon	Prayer
12:15 p.m.	Goal setting
12:25 p.m.	Weekly schedule evaluation
12:35 p.m.	Calendar planning
1:05 p.m.	Kickoff event brainstorming
1:20 p.m.	Budget report and discussion
1:30 p.m.	Planning next year's group projects
1:45 p.m.	Publicity report and discussion
2:00 p.m.	GLO evaluation and ideas
2:15 p.m.	Ministry team evaluations
2:35 p.m.	Ministry team brainstorming
3:05 p.m.	Registration ideas
3:20 p.m.	Luncheon evaluations
3:35 p.m.	Luncheon ideas
4:05 p.m.	Fellowship class evaluations
4:25 p.m.	Fellowship class ideas
5:00 p.m.	Dismissal prayer

The Scheduling Process

The process of calendaring an entire year is tedious but well worth the effort.

In the model women's ministry, the calendar year for women's ministry began in August and ended in May. It consisted of a fall and spring semester. Dividing your women's ministry year into two semesters provides easy entry points for newcomers and provides movement of women to enhance fellowship and prevent monotony.

Let's walk through a five-step process to schedule a year of women's ministry. Use a large calendar for the planning process.

Step 1. Beginning and ending dates. Our fall semester begins on Thursday after public schools start and ends on the first Thursday of December. Similarly, the spring semester begins on Thursday following school beginning in January and finalizes on the first week of May. Use the school calendar to determine a starting and ending date for both semesters. Mark them on the calendar. If a school holiday occurs on a meeting day, women's ministry does not meet, so X through those dates.

The story continues . . .

When we first began LIGHT, we scheduled meetings through the month of May. Our attendance was great, right up through the early May luncheon. The remaining weeks of May were sparsely attended. That same nosedive in attendance happened every year.

Voilà! A brilliant member of our women's leadership team suggested a new plan. The luncheon on the first week of May would mark the grand finale. This would accommodate women's schedules, eliminate the dip-in-attendance weeks, and end on a high note. It worked perfectly.

As my Granny would say, "Don't beat a dead horse!" Pay attention to the schedules and availability of women in your church and create a schedule that enhances attendance.

Step 2. Kickoff events. The first meeting of both the fall and spring semesters is set aside for fellowship, introduction, and registration. The August kickoff is huge; January's more subdued. Mark those two dates as kickoff dates (see chapter 7).

Step 3. Special events. Determine dates for women's events, such as retreats, conferences, and luncheons. In our women's ministry, we scheduled four luncheons each year. One luncheon was on the first Thursday of December, one on the first Thursday of May. Mark those luncheon dates. The other luncheons occurred half-way between the kickoff date and the end-of-semester luncheon, providing an easy entry point for newcomers at mid-semester. Select a midpoint date for the spring and fall semester, and mark them as luncheon dates. The regular women's ministry program of ministry teams and classes did not meet on luncheon days.

When scheduling luncheons, consider significant events on your church calendar as well. For example, if your church plans a spring revival, it may be advantageous to schedule the luncheon to coincide with that week.

Step 4. Regular meeting days. Now that you've determined the beginning and ending dates and the luncheon dates for fall and spring semesters, count the remaining days between those to determine class lengths. By dividing each semester into two sessions, you have created several easy entry points for newcomers. You will be amazed at how many guests at a mid-semester luncheon will enthusiastically register for a new ceramics class or Bible study that begins the next week.

For example, if a semester has twelve women's ministry meeting days (excluding kickoff and luncheons), some fellowship classes, such as *Experiencing God* Bible study, will last for twelve weeks. Others, such as a ceramics class, may last six weeks. Attempt to offer at least one half-semester choice to provide an entry point for newcomers at mid-semester.

Step 5. Schedule other dates. Pencil in dates for group projects, leadership meetings, and any other events. For example, if you want to plan an informal picnic with women and children in the spring, put it on the calendar. If the group project for fall is a cookbook, write recipe deadlines, submission dates, and book release dates. If the ministry coordinator plans a lunch for ministry team leaders, put it on the calendar. Every topic discussed during the meeting is added to the master calendar.

Make a copy of the tentative calendar for each officer, and submit it to the church office for approval. This process of creating an entire year's calendar will be repeated each spring for the next calendar year. Planning ahead will pay big dividends.

A word about planning: Admittedly, your first-year planning is unique. A sample time line is given as a general guideline. Don't fret! This process will be simplified enormously for subsequent years.

Sample Planning Calendar

2010-2011
L.I.G H.T. CALENDAR

LIGHT meets Thursday 9:30 to Noon
Luncheons 11:30-1PM

AUGUST
14
LIGHT KICKOFF
21
LIGHT CLASSES/MINISTRIES
28
LIGHT CLASSES/MINISTRIES

SEPTEMBER
4
LIGHT CLASSES/MINISTRIES
11
LIGHT CLASSES/MINISTRIES
18
LIGHT CLASSES/MINISTRIES
25
LIGHT CLASSES/MINISTRIES

OCTOBER
2
LIGHT LUNCHEON
9
LIGHT CLASSES/MINISTRIES
16
LIGHT CLASSES/MINISTRIES
23
LIGHT CLASSES/MINISTRIES
30
LIGHT CLASSES/MINISTRIES

NOVEMBER
6
LIGHT CLASSES/MINISTRIES
13
LIGHT CLASSES/MINISTRIES
20
SPECIAL MISSIONS CLASS
    AND MINISTRIES

DEC 4
LIGHT LUNCHEON

JANUARY
8
SPRING LIGHT KICKOFF
15
LIGHT CLASSES/MINISTRIES
22
LIGHT CLASSES/MINISTRIES
29
LIGHT CLASSES/MINISTRIES

FEBRUARY
5
LIGHT CLASSES/MINISTRIES
12
LIGHT CLASSES/MINISTRIES
19
LIGHT CLASSES/MINISTRIES
26
LIGHT CLASSES/MINISTRIES

MARCH
5
LIGHT LUNCHEON
19
LIGHT CLASSES/MINISTRIES
26
LIGHT CLASSES/MINISTRIES

APRIL
2
LIGHT CLASSES/MINISTRIES
9
LIGHT CLASSES/MINISTRIES
16
LIGHT CLASSES/MINISTRIES
23
LIGHT CLASSES/MINISTRIES
30
LIGHT CLASSES/MINISTRIES

MAY 7
LIGHT LUNCHEON

Bright NightLIGHT

A small church in Indiana began a NightLIGHT last fall. They were absolutely ecstatic when forty women attended the fall sessions. Their leaders rave about the impact it has on women in their church, and their pastor is thrilled with the results. Their second semester has just begun, and interest is higher than ever.

Select a time that you feel will best involve leaders and other women in your church.

Time Line for Beginning a Women's Ministry

5 months ahead	• Meet with pastor to determine need. • Do an all-church survey. • Recruit ministry team coordinator.
4 months ahead	• Recruit remaining officers. • Approve dates, times, and overall plan with pastor. • Officers meet to pray and plan. • Officers begin recruiting class leaders and assistants.
3 months ahead	• Ministry team leaders begin to develop their plans. • Officers finalize teams and plans for their areas. • "Soft" publicity begins.
2 months ahead	• Publicity blitz begins. • Complete ministry/class descriptions submitted for brochure. • Finalize kickoff event details. • Order needed materials for Bible studies, Women on Mission, etc.
1 month ahead	• Kickoff invitation and women's ministry brochure mailed to every female member and prospect. • In-church publicity accelerates. • Room assignments are made. • Individual teams meet for final planning as needed.
3 weeks ahead	• Begin major publicity blitz. • Print registration forms.
2 weeks ahead	• Make announcement in the worship service. • Contact every female member by phone.
1 week ahead	• Send e-invitations or notes to those without e-mail.
1 day ahead	• Complete setup for kickoff. • Officers and leaders meet for prayer.

CHAPTER 7

The Kickoff Event

Those who come in may see the light.

—Luke 8:16

It's the "event of the year." Kind of like opening day at the ballpark, college orientation, or seeing the new models at the auto show. The kickoff event is the unveiling of a new semester of your church's women's ministry. A fantastic beginning can set the stage for a successful, fruitful women's ministry program in your church.

For the first meeting of the fall and spring semesters, ladies gather en masse for fellowship and registration, and no one wants to miss out. Your leadership team will put as much time and effort into this one morning event as they invest in the rest of the year, but it's worth it.

Fresh Start

When we first began a women's ministry at our church, my marketing background told me the importance of that first event. First impressions count. A big, happy crowd at an opening event would predict a big happy crowd for the weekly program. I did not, however, understand the ongoing importance of a kickoff event for *each* semester.

Every semester's kickoff event will be unique. Our fall kickoff was a huge event, and the January kickoff was slightly more subdued. It may be a formal tea or a fair. It could be an ice cream social, a road rally, or a lunch. But one thing's for sure: it's always a first-class shebang. Women who attend are informed about all areas of the women's ministries and eager to spread the word to their friends. They will enjoy great fellowship and get a glimpse of the exciting ministries, classes, and friendships awaiting them each semester.

Unless the kickoff is a luncheon, it should be scheduled at the exact hour and day of the week as the women's ministry will meet each week. Since our church's LIGHT met at 9:30 a.m. on Thursdays, that was our kickoff day and time. The kick-off will usually last only an hour or an hour and a half.

Don't forget the importance of friendly greeters. As first-time guests arrive at a kickoff, a greeter should accompany them inside and introduce them to a regular attender who can help them feel comfortable.

A volunteer photographer should take lots of photographs to use for Sunday's preservice audiovisuals, posters, publicity, history scrapbook, future brochures, and photo reports.

Why "waste" the first day of a new semester's women's ministry with a kickoff event? You'll find it's worthwhile for a variety of reasons:

- *The buzz factor.* Women will discover all of the semester's classes and ministry teams. Everyone will be talking about it both before and after the wonderful event. And that's good gossip. Isn't it great when people are excited about God's work?

- *The registration factor.* A focus of the kickoff will be introduction and registration for all the semester's choices for ministry teams, Bible classes, missions groups, crafts classes, luncheons, and special ladies' events. All the paperwork is done, and you're ready to begin women's ministry the next week.

- *Easy-entry-point factor.* It's an ideal place for newcomers and guests to join in and participate. Because everything's new, it's less intimidating for out-siders to check it out.

- *The fellowship factor.* I admit it. It is a social event. Newcomers meet friends, and all the ladies are excited to see one another after the summer or Christmas break.

The preevent publicity must be wow quality and quantity. Every female church member and recent church guest should receive multiple invitations: verbal, mailed, e-mailed, bulletin, newsletter, posters, announcements. Fellowship classes and ministry teams may be enumerated on some publicity pieces to entice newcomers to attend.

Small Church Tip

- This is a great time to think big! Plan a fun-themed kickoff, but scale it down slightly to fit your group and their guests.

- You've planned the entire year's schedule and know it's going to be worth attending. Put great effort into publicity for the kickoff, and plan to include many new women.

- One advantage of a small group is that some kickoffs may be planned at a member's home or local site.

- Encourage each church member to bring a friend to the kickoff. The event and women's ministry plans will be so inviting, they'll come back.

- A small group could combine the kickoff with a group ministry activity such as going as a group for a nursing home or shut-in visit.

Elements of a Kickoff Event

Though no two kickoff events look just alike, each includes the same four elements:

1. A unique theme
2. Fellowship time
3. Food
4. Semester preview and registration

A Unique Theme

All year long your leadership team will be brainstorming ideas for next semester's kickoff event. The event may be planned by the officers, or they may designate a separate group to plan (see sample kick off invitation on page 62). As they prayerfully select a unique theme, every detail can be built around it—the publicity, the decor, the program, food presentation, favors, and music. By planning months ahead of time, you'll be amazed at how the pieces will fit together.

Although the purpose remains the same, the actual presentation of the ministry and class offerings is different for each kickoff. Here are a dozen sample theme ideas:

HOUSE SLIPPER TEA

It's a spoof on a high tea event, and it's great fun. The tea can be held at the church or in a member's home. There are flowers and scones and china and silver, but the dress is casual, and ladies are encouraged to wear house slippers. Ministry teams and fellowship classes have elegant displays, and extra slippers are provided at the entry for those who forget theirs.

LIGHT's IN FASHION

Treat it like a hoopla fashion show! Build a ribbon runway, play background music, and write a great script for the announcer to describe the models. Each model represents a ministry or class and is dressed to illustrate it. For example, the nursing home team leader could push a wheelchair with a comical "patient" who alternately knits and snores. The welcome ministry team leader could carry a big basket of welcome bags and an open city map. Conclude the program with a dramatic interpretation of an illustrative song such as "Can Anybody See Her?"

ROAD RALLY

Recruit every member of your church who has an SUV or van to drive for this event. As ladies arrive, they receive a colored paper key. After coffee, use a megaphone to welcome them to the road rally. Instruct ladies to follow the woman with the same color key as theirs to their assigned road rally car. Each group follows a map, rather like a scavenger hunt. They drive to every place in the community where weekly ministry teams will go. For example, the map could take them to the hospital, nursing home, a shut-in's home, a staged newcomer's home, or the benevolence closet. At each site that ministry team leader is waiting outside to give each road rally participant a note about that ministry team. The last stop on the map is the city park or the church lawn where red checked tablecloths hold sumptuous picnic baskets with brunch.

JAVA LIGHT

A coffee-tasting event could capitalize on today's coffee craze. Order inexpensive imprinted LIGHT coffee mugs for favors and serve different flavors or types of hot or cold coffees at each display for classes or ministry teams. Talk to a local coffee shop about sponsoring your event. Ladies view exhibits of classes and ministries as they sample drinks and snacks.

A TECHNO SHOWCASE

Use all varieties of audiovisuals at various booths to introduce the semester's choices. The program features videotaped interviews to introduce the leaders and show ministry teams in action last semester. Use PowerPoint to present details for ministry teams and classes. Consider how you can use headphones, cell phones, PDA, or iPods in a skit or presentation.

RECIPE FOR MINISTRY

Kickoff your women's ministry semester and unveil your church cookbook with a tasting event. Serve one food recipe from the cookbook at each class or ministry display table. For the program introduce ministry teams and classes in the form of a recipe. For example, "Stir in one cup of hospital ministry. This team is led by Jeannie Dunn."

A LIGHT FAIR

A carnival or fair theme can feature a colorful booth for each ministry team or class with an interactive display or game about their plans. For example, the missions class booth could have a "guess how many international missionaries our church supports" contest, with a jelly-bean jar holding that number of jelly beans. (Currently a Southern Baptist church would have 5,320 jellybeans.) Use balloons, a giant tent, carousel music, and carnival snacks.

REAL COOL POOL PARTY

This kickoff event takes place poolside at a church member's home. Gather around the cabana for banana slush punch, fruit kabobs, displays under umbrellas, and a casual introductory event.

Light Your World

Use all kinds of lamps and lights as centerpieces. Serve a light (calorie) menu. If possible, plan a moment in the program where all lights are extinguished and a single match is struck to illustrate how just one light can make a difference in darkness. Or stage a fashion show with each leader carrying a different type light on the runway, such as a lantern, a candle, a lamp, and a flashlight. Emphasize how ministry teams can shine light in your community.

A LIGHT Kickoff

Use a football theme complete with goalposts and your "starting lineup" (leaders) in jerseys. Print listings of classes and ministry teams in a playbook format. Use a local team's colors or your women's ministry color scheme, have a silly skit of unlikely cheerleaders leading a women's ministry cheer, use band instruments for music, and create a subdued pep-rally atmosphere.

My Favorite Hat

It's a formal event with fancy foods and froufrou decor. Invite ladies to wear a hat and provide extra hats for those who forget. A hat fashion show could introduce each leader of a ministry team or class, and ladies could be challenged to "choose your hat" (select your class and ministry team) as they register.

Hop to It or Leap into LIGHT

At this frog-themed event, officers and leaders wear green, and only green food and drinks are served. The program, titled "Hopping Lessons," could feature brief testimonies about ministry teams' adventures from last semester. Take it a step further with a green fashion show featuring ministry team leaders, with audiotaped testimonies playing as they are introduced. If ladies at your church can take a joke, freeze plastic flies in ice cubes for their drinks. Make a point that what's desirable for some (frogs love flies) may not thrill others, so you're offering lots of choices of classes and ministry teams.

Every theme will not require extravagant decorations, but the entry area should be stunning, the food presentation should be memorable, and the podium area should be attractively decorated.

Consider preparing a memento to fit the theme such as a bookmark, a magnet, or a small handcrafted item. For example, at our "fair" themed kickoff, we ordered four-inch, bright pink LIGHT buttons. A volunteer walked around during the fair, distributing the buttons from a flat box strapped to her shoulders, reminiscent of old theater or sports events concessions. Another year we ordered tiny writing pens that looked like a match and were imprinted with "LIGHT your world!"

As your leadership team prayerfully plans ahead and brainstorms together, you'll be able to come up with better themes than these! Enjoy the theme-building process.

Fellowship Time

Never overlook the importance of informal fellowship time during a kickoff day. How do you legislate fellowship during an event? Think about it: many friends have not seen one another for much of the summer or Christmas break. Newcomers will be present, eager to make new acquaintances.

Carefully consider how your schedule can include time for conversation and friendship-building. This will often occur during a coffee and snack time as women arrive. Leaders set the pace for fellowship by informally introducing people to one another as they arrive. Recorded or live music sets a nice background, and by providing only a few chairs, ladies will naturally move around and interact with one another.

Food

The menu for your kickoff event may often be influenced by the event theme. Refreshments can be as simple as coffee and cookies or as extravagant as a four-course luncheon.

A kickoff event is not an appropriate venue for potluck or carry-in dishes, which might negatively impact attendance. It would be appropriate, however, for the event planning team to bring food. For example, our leadership team once prepared brunch menu items. Each person used clear glass dishes, and the presentation was lovely.

In addition to other drinks, fill a punch bowl with ice, water, and lime slices. It's always a hit.

Food presentation is important. For example, a high tea demands china cups. A fair theme may serve popcorn and cola in paper cups. A picnic theme may serve cold chicken and potato salad on paper plates from picnic baskets with red-checked cloths.

Some kickoffs may use a color scheme for decor or food. Food and drinks at a January winter-themed event could all be white. A carnival-themed event might use a red and yellow decorating color scheme. Colorful details, such as a silk scarf or fabric square, can enhance tables.

Fresh flowers enhance any event. Flowers from leaders' gardens could be strewn between food dishes to create a lovely buffet. Use ivy from someone's yard. Try pine branches during winter. Set boxes of varying heights beneath tablecloths, and display food at different levels.

Plan ahead to avoid long lines for food service. If food is presented buffet-style, serve from both sides of the table. Set up multiple food and drink stations around a room so guests must move around to gather their refreshments.

Semester Preview and Registration

All the rest is really fluff! This is what the day is all about. Ladies who attend the kickoff event will learn about your church's women's ministry for that semester and register for classes and ministry teams. Choices will be presented in both printed and visual forms. The program can include artistic elements, visual interest, top quality music, and an upbeat presentation. Create a printed schedule for those who will speak during the program. Invite the pastor's wife to take a part in the program. She could welcome the group or lead a closing prayer. Avoid tedious announcements and details by printing those details for distribution. Our kickoff events usually last an hour and a half or less.

The event theme will help determine how to present the semester preview and how to register. Women will select their classes and ministry teams for the semester at this event. Craft classes will provide supply lists. Bible studies and mission groups will provide study books for purchase at cost. Leaders may even provide assignments for the first day of class.

Choices of ministry teams are presented either dramatically or visually. For many themes a display table will be prepared by each ministry team leader and fellowship class leader. The ministry team tables may have photographs of last semester's ministry and a handout sheet to describe the ministry. Each is decorated specifically to tell about that ministry, so a welcome ministry team table may have maps of the area where they welcome newcomers, samples of the welcome packets they deliver, and perhaps even a wireless doorbell or a standup door in a casing. The display for a Bible study would have a Bible and a study book displayed and a signup sheet to order the study guides. A craft class could display samples of the finished product and provide a complete list of needed supplies for the class. A mission study group could display upcoming topics of study, maps of missionary locations, and missionary newsletters. The goal of the displays is to entice ladies to attend that class or participate in that ministry team.

After ladies have previewed all their choices, they are invited to register for the semester. The method of registration will also fit your theme.

For example, an "It's in the Bag" kickoff event features a leader from each ministry team or class in a fashion show of purses, pausing at the end of the runway to pull something out of the bag to represent their ministry. Onlookers would have a ballot-type registration form, listing every choice of activities. As they view the show and listen to the announcer describe classes and ministry teams that are illustrated, ladies check their choices on their "ballot" and fill in their contact information on the reverse side. Hostesses collect the registration ballots as ladies leave.

A "fair" themed kickoff could have a fun, interactive booth for each class and ministry team option with a clipboard where viewers can register for that group. At the exit a huge wall board lists all the ministry teams and classes, and each lady signs below the groups where she registered.

Another kickoff could use a punch card. Attenders receive a hole punch at each display as they pass by. At the bottom of the card, they write their name and their choice of a ministry team and a class, and then turn in the completed registration punch card for a door prize drawing.

No matter how the semester preview is presented and registration occurs, the final result of the kickoff should be a complete listing of those planning to attend each class and ministry team this semester. After the kickoff event a roster is compiled, and each leader makes a personal contact with her class or team members before the first day of women's ministry.

Ascertain that the meeting area is perfectly clean and inviting. If it needs fresh paint, obtain permission, buy a bucket of paint, and have a paint party before kickoff day. Set up more chairs than you expect. Print more handouts than you think you'll need, and encourage attenders to take an extra handout to a friend.

Provide a signup sheet for volunteers to bring snacks one day during the semester. Invite ladies to purchase tickets for upcoming luncheons, ladies' retreat, or other ladies' events at your church. Ask ladies to print their name on their registration form exactly as they prefer for the name tag, and let them know name tags will be ready for pickup on the first meeting day. Distribute a semester calendar with a magnet attached (see page 45). Take a quick photo as each person arrives for a photo directory.

Through careful planning and attention to detail, your leadership team will craft an unforgettable kickoff event. And you'll wonder how next year's kickoff day could ever match up.

But it will.

And ladies will show up.

And ladies will be challenged.

And ladies will get busy about God's work.

It's worth the effort.

Sample Kickoff Invitation

CHAPTER 8

The Friendship Factor

I was a stranger and you took Me in.
—Matthew 25:35

In our program the hospitality coordinator has responsibility for all the details we'll discuss in this chapter. She will intentionally plan ways to help women build Christian friendships. It begins at the registration desk and continues after dismissal. In this chapter you'll read ideas for name tags, registration, directory, prayer partners, and the coffee break—all part of the friendship factor.

An important element of women's ministry is friendship-building. Take this pop quiz.

Which of the following best describes the "friendship factor" of your women's ministry?

❑ *The country club.* The "us four and no more" mentality. Great entertainment for ourselves. Guests who fit our standards are welcome to come and watch us. We might even allow them to join.

❏ *Synchronized swimming.* It's every woman for herself. We'll work hard side by side but with little interaction or friendship-building. Guests may swim alongside.

❏ *Koinonia Christian fellowship.* Intentional planning goes into creating an atmosphere of fellowship. Everyone is included and loved. Women who attend will find new friends.

Quote from Survey (woman in her forties)

"My favorite thing about LIGHT is meeting new people. That has been wonderful! I've met people of every age I would never have gotten to know otherwise."

The Registration Desk

The registration area is attractive, neat, and clean. It often boasts a vase of flowers from someone's garden or a seasonal decoration. Though lots of women are coming in, there is no long line or confusion. Registration is a difficult responsibility, but a good hospitality coordinator makes it appear simple. She designs the registration form that ladies complete at the kickoff event (sample on page 69). She compiles those names for a weekly sign-in form (see page 67) and reprints it weekly to include newcomers. There is a simple, systematic plan for ladies to register their attendance as they arrive. They simply check their name, take an announcement sheet, and head for their class.

Got the picture? Rather than creating a bottleneck, registration sends ladies right in for the blessing awaiting them. A separate table holds registration forms for a first-time guest, and her contact information is relayed to her class and ministry team leader.

Add Flowers

No, this is not your top priority in planning a women's ministry, but it's a nice addition. Watch for ways to add flowers. Some examples:

- If someone in your group has a flower garden, she may volunteer to bring a few cut flowers weekly for the registration or snack table.
- For a buffet served on several levels, the decorating team could bring vines and flowers from their gardens to intersperse around food. Gorgeous!
- Lots of zinnias or roses in your garden? Deliver one to each homebound or nursing home visit.
- A decorating team could gather wildflowers for centerpieces.
- Encourage members to purchase garage sale vases. Ministry teams can deliver flowers left from Sunday or brought from home.

Greeters

Greeters set the pace for a great morning. Highly visible signs direct women from the parking lot to the meeting area, where greeters welcome each attender. Your church's friendliest ladies serve as greeters, and they take their responsibility seriously. Greeters arrive well before the first attender. They dress attractively to make a good first impression and share a smile with every woman who arrives. A warm greeting is a valuable gift. For some women this may be their only hug for the week!

When the hospitality coordinator recruits greeters, she may invite all of them to her home for lunch and a brief training session. By planning ahead, they'll know how to handle latecomers, newcomers, and old-timers.

Every person who arrives is greeted, but when a newcomer arrives, the greeter gives her full attention. She remembers the guest's name, helps her with registration, and escorts her to class where she introduces the guest to new friends. She finds and visits with the guest during the fellowship coffee break and writes a note to thank her for attending.

The story continues . . .

I saw her through the church window before she opened the door, and my heart skipped a beat. She wore an ultratight miniskirt, a bouffant hair style, heavy makeup, and a tiny butterfly tattoo on her shoulder. *How will the women treat this stranger?* I wondered, and shot up a silent prayer for God's grace.

I was never prouder of our greeters than in those next minutes. Their warm welcome was genuine, and as Miranda registered for LIGHT, she was surrounded by new friends, accepting her with God's love.

She stopped by the ladies' room before class, and I temporarily forgot about her. When Miranda emerged from the restroom, arm in arm with Betty, she was smiling from ear to ear. Now you must get this picture. Betty is a gray-haired, sprightly woman, the wife of the town's mayor, and a soul-winner. She chirped, "Miranda, tell Diana what just happened!"

Tears filled my eyes as Miranda told how she met Betty while she washed her hands in the restroom. Their conversation turned toward spiritual things, and they sat on the sofa to chat. When Betty asked if she had a personal relationship with Jesus Christ, Miranda begged her to explain how she could know Him. She prayed a prayer of forgiveness and commitment to Christ!

In upcoming weeks Miranda was baptized as a new believer. She was encircled and discipled by new Christian friends, and she brought many other women to meet Christ.

It's not enough to have a nice program and do good deeds. It's all about telling a lost world about God's plan for their life. LIGHT your world.

Small Church Tip

Carefully evaluate the first impression of newcomers. Is your entrance perfectly clean and well lit? Will a friendly member call to thank the guest for attending? Will members welcome a guest who attends? Remember: if no one new is included in your women's ministry, it's just a club!

Sample Weekly Sign-in Form

LIGHT Attendance

NAME	8/23	9/8	9/13	9/20	9/27	10/11	10/18	10/25	11/1	11/8	11/15	11/29
Abernathy, Gena	X	X	X									
Bard, Marta	X		X									
Butler, Joan	X	X	X									
Cinder, Marian	X	X	X									
Ellis, Janet	X	X	X									
Garvin, Anna		X										
Irvey, Karen	X	X										
Kirk, Kimberly	X	X										
Kokat, Nelda	X	X	X									
Lindley, Rea			X									
Mann, Burt	X	X	X									
Moore, Kaye	X	X	X									
Nanney, Fran	X		X									
Noble, Jan	X		X									
Pippin, Donna	X	X	X									
Ray, Jennifer	X	X										
Render, Jonna	X		X									
Remington, Rosemary	X	X	X									
Reynolds, Linda	X	X										
Roach, Linda	X	X	X									
Trayner, Ulla	X	X	X									

Ten Tips for Greeting a Newcomer

1. Don't make her wander around. Clear directional signs lead her from the church entrance to the women's ministry meeting area.
2. Greeters are waiting at the door. Each person who attends is welcomed, and greeters give newcomers their undivided attention.
3. A large sign reads, "Welcome to LIGHT."
4. Registration is simple. A greeter escorts her to a separate registration table for guests and helps her select a class and ministry team. If classes have begun, she's escorted to her class, and a greeter returns for her form.
5. The guest receives a temporary name tag. She is informed that her permanent name tag will be prepared by next week.
6. The newcomer is given a women's ministry program, a women's ministry directory, a church newsletter, a women's ministry newsletter, and an announcement sheet.
7. The greeter personally escorts the guest to her class, introduces her to some ladies, and asks one woman to escort her to coffee break after class.
8. The ministry team leader chosen by the newcomer is notified of her new team member so she can watch for her and plan accordingly.
9. The guest's name is written on the whiteboard, and she is welcomed during the coffee break.
10. During the next few days, the guest will receive a call, note, or e-mail from the greeter, hospitality coordinator, fellowship class leader, and ministry team leader. Each will try to remember her name, recognize her at church, and call her by name next week.

Bonus: First-time are were usually invited to join a smaller group of women for lunch after women's ministry.

LIGHT
Fall 2009 REGISTRATION

Name _____ E-mail _____

Address _____ Zip _____

Home phone _____ Alternate phone _____

Member of Hope Baptist? ❏ Yes ❏ No Birthday (mo/day) _____

Preschool children who will attend child care _____

EnLIGHTening Classes
(Circle one for each session)

Session I (August 31—September 28)

Women on Mission—missions class
First Place—weight Bible class
Beginning quilting—craft class
The Strong Willed Child—moms' Bible study
How Much Is Enough?—financial Bible study
A Heart Like His—Beth Moore Bible study

Session II (October 12—December 7)

Heaven: Your Real Home—Bible study
Making angels—craft and Bible class
Women on Mission—missions class
1-day Christmas projects—crafts class
Building Blocks of Faith—parent Bible study
First Place, continued
A Heart Like His, continued

MINISTRY TEAMS
(Circle one for semester)

Food Pantry and Clothes Closet
Hospital Team
Nursing Home Team
Love Crafts Team
Welcome Wagon Team
Meals on Wheels Team
Prison Bible Correspondence
Quill Team
Homebound Team
Cradle Roll Team
Christmas House Benevolence
Prayer Walk Plus Team

Sample Registration Form

Name Tags

Name tags are an important element of a women's ministry. In our model women's ministry, plastic, engraved name badges were ordered from an office supply store for every member. The church name was across the top, the woman's name was printed in very large letters in the middle, and the words "Ladies Intentionally Going, Helping, and Touching" printed across the bottom. They were snazzy-looking name tags, and ladies were proud to wear them.

At the kickoff event, ladies printed their names on the registration form exactly as they wanted it on their name tags. They checked their preference for clip-on or pin attachment hardware. Name tags were ordered after the kickoff event and were ready for the first day of women's ministry. Women were encouraged to wear their name tags faithfully.

The budget allotted to women's ministry was used to purchase the name tags, and it was an excellent investment. We used the same name tags each semester. When ladies misplaced their name tags, we asked that they pay for its replacement. Some ladies ordered a backup name badge.

When a newcomer attended, we informed her that she would have an official name tag awaiting her next week. The hospitality coordinator would e-mail the weekly order to the business supply store, and newcomers immediately felt included.

Five Reasons for Permanent Name Tags

1. Name tags enhance friendships. It's easier to learn names with a prompt.
2. Name tags add professionalism and identity. When women saturate your community for ministry, they'll be noticed. Name tags lend legitimacy when ladies are visiting new move-ins, nursing homes, prisons, or hospitals.
3. Name tags enhance ministry. The homebound friend or hospital patient immediately knows your name. Benevolence ministry is personalized.
4. Name tags help identify first-time guests. They're the women with disposable name tags.
5. Name tags help newcomers fit in. When a newcomer knows she'll receive her official name tag next week, she realizes that she is truly welcome.

Women's Ministry Directory

A directory is not an absolute necessity, but since one important goal of your women's ministry is to encourage Christian friendship, it's worth the effort. Your directory can be as simple as a spreadsheet with basic information such as name, phone, e-mail address, and ministry team. (Note: once again, we're keeping ministry as a priority.) A member with computer skills will enjoy the opportunity to use her gifts in this manner.

Even better, use a digital camera to take a quick head shot of each member on the first day of women's ministry, add name, phone, and e-mail address for each person, and print a simple black-and-white directory on the office copier. Include the pastor's name, name and address of the church, and church Web site address on the cover. Women will use it constantly, and fellowship will be enhanced.

First-time guests receive a directory, and an add-on page is distributed each month with newcomers' information.

Prayer Partners

Assign mentors or prayer partners, inviting ladies to pray for that person for the entire year. The assignment is simple and does not require a large commitment. We varied the assignment method each year.

For example, one year we took a digital photo of each woman as she arrived at women's ministry. While ladies were in fellowship classes, magnets were attached to the back of the photos. Chairs in the coffee break area were arranged in groups of two, photos were randomly placed in chairs, and when ladies came for coffee, each met her prayer partner, exchanged photos, and visited together during the break.

One year we called our prayer partners "heart-to-heart." An assignment team paired prayer partners, attempting to put an older and younger woman who had a common denominator, such as interest or address. Other years prayer partners were made by simply asking women to select someone they didn't know very well, visit during that day's coffee break, and commit to pray for her during the rest of the year.

It doesn't have to be complicated, but prayer partners often become friends. It's worth the effort.

Quote from Survey

Question: How can we improve friendship-building at LIGHT?
Answer: "Can't improve! I've made more friends at LIGHT than I've ever had in my life!"

Extracurricular Fellowship Ideas

Plan optional friendship-building elements each year, such as a summer mission trip, an annual ladies' retreat or conference, or a picnic in the park. Ministry team leaders could plan a brown-bag lunch once each semester for their team members. Many women may informally meet others at a restaurant for lunch after women's ministry. Some churches serve a weekly salad lunch after women's ministry. Create informal fellowship opportunities.

 **Coffee Fellowship**
10:30 to 10:45
All Together Now

The Fellowship Coffee Break

Oh, yes. There's more value in the coffee break than just caffeine! If the fellowship classes are "for me" and the ministry teams are "for Him," then the coffee break is "for us." The exclusive purpose is friendship-building—pure, simple Christian fellowship. Women need time to laugh together, to show photos of their grandchild or new baby, to exchange recipes, to chat about God's blessings.

In our model women's ministry, women from all the different classes meet together for a short coffee break before leaving for ministry teams. Leaders of each fellowship class dismiss promptly and lead the way to the coffee, so everyone arrives at once.

Choose a large room near the fellowship classes for the coffee break. The hospitality coordinator's team sets a lovely table, using fresh flowers or seasonal décor and pretty napkins. Food is ready to serve when fellowship classes arrive. To avoid congestion and encourage mingling, the serving table is across the room from the drinks, and a few sparse chairs are available.

Women signed up at the kickoff to bring finger food snacks. In addition to coffee and juice, serve a punch bowl or glass pitcher of iced water with lemon slices.

After fifteen minutes of informal fellowship and snacks, the women's ministry coordinator rings a bell, acknowledges newcomers, and leads a prayer for ministry teams before dismissing. A laminated sign for each ministry team is hung on the walls to help women find their team before they leave for ministry. Announcements are rarely verbalized; they are prepared ahead of time as handout sheets or written on a whiteboard.

In our model women's ministry, the dismissal varied each semester. Most semesters we simply invited women to gather in a large circle or in a small circle with their ministry team before we closed in prayer. A few semesters we planned a brief send-off. For example, each week of one semester featured a videotaped testimony from a different ministry team. Another semester we planned "ninety-second devotionals" led by staff wives, deacon wives, and other leaders. It's surprising how powerful a ninety-second devotional can be. We used a piano metronome as a tongue-in-cheek timer.

Other semesters we selected a theme song, joined hands in a huge circle, and dismissed with the song (sample song on page 74).

We presented a "Shiner Award" each week of one semester. Ministry team leaders submitted a paragraph-long nomination story about a member's involvement in ministry. Just before the closing prayer, we announced the winner of the award each week and read the descriptive paragraph. The trophy was hilarious—a lightbulb glued to a board with "Shiner Award" scribbled in marker. It was hokey but fun. Years later I visited a church member's lovely mansion, and there on her marble fireplace stood her Shiner Award!

For one coffee break each year, we planned a neighborhood coffee break. This takes significant preparation and lasts the entire coffee break, but it's worthwhile. Mark the physical home address of each regular attender on a city map and draw a circle around subdivisions or natural barriers to assign women in small neighborhood groups. We grouped chairs, with each woman's name on a chair, and women enjoyed fellowship with their neighbors.

After the closing prayer, ladies gather with their ministry teams. In just minutes the room is empty, and women are ministering in God's name all across the community.

Nothing Trivial about Fellowship

It sounds trivial, I know, but looking over several years' worth of evaluations, I'm reminded again of the importance of friendship-making and fellowship. Though the weekly coffee break lasts only a few minutes, the social aspects are enormous.

If you're reading this book, you're probably a leader-type person with plenty of buddies at church. But, believe it or not, the majority of women who will be coming to women's ministry do not have lots of friends at church. And they're looking for meaningful friendships.

Fellow Laborers

As women pray, plan, study, and serve together, friendships develop. I must admit that my best friends in life were developed as we ministered together. As we planned a retreat or prayed for a missionary or visited the sick, we became dear friends. The ministry teams and fellowship classes provide a great way to make lifelong Christian friends.

Jesus Loves Through Me
by Randy Lind

I'll let my light shine everywhere I go,
I'll let my light shine so all the world will know,
I'll let my light shine for all the world to see
That Jesus loves them,
Jesus loves them,
Jesus loves through me.

Score available in the resource section for duplication on page 178.
Used by permission.

CHAPTER 9

Ministry Teams

She was always doing good works and acts of charity.
—Acts 9:36

Ah, the heart of effective women's ministry: the ministry teams! If your current weekly women's ministry plan is inwardly focused, this chapter may revolutionize your entire program.

Remember my story at the first of this book when I'd asked those ten women's ministry leaders the same question, "If you were beginning all over again to create the quality women's ministry in your church, what one element would you change?" Their answer was, "I would focus on ministry." Hands-on ministry can change your church's reputation. It can change the hearts of women in your church. It can add excitement and a purposeful witness. And it can change your women's ministry from a me-me-me mantra to an others-focused "go ye" purpose.

In our model LIGHT women's ministry program, the weekly plan included three parts with three purposes:

Fellowship Class hour—"for me"
Coffee Fellowship time—"for us"
Ministry Team hour—"for Him!"

This is the "for Him" chapter. Oh, yes, it's all really about Him, and the ministry teams will challenge women to "be doers of the word and not hearers only" (James 1:22).

Examples of Ministry Teams

*"Let your light shine before men, so that they may see your good works
and give glory to your Father in heaven." Matthew 5:16*

Ministry Team	Matthew 25	Purpose
Hospital ministry team	v. 36	Visit hospital patients
Welcome ministry team	v. 35	Deliver welcome gift packet to invite newcomers to church
Homebound ministry team	v. 36	Visit shut-ins by appointment
Prison Bible correspondence (or prison team)	v. 36	Grade Bible studies for Christian prison organization
Clothes closet benevolence ministry team	v. 36	Collect, sort, and distribute used clothing
Outreach ministry team	v. 35	Make outreach visits to recent church guests for evangelism
Nursing home ministry team	v. 36	Visit in local nursing home

English as second language class	v. 35	Provide Bible-based English classes for immigrants
New mommy ministry team	v. 35	Visit, deliver packets, pray
Farming ministry team	v. 35	Contact and minister to residents in a specific neighborhood for outreach
Food pantry team	v. 35	Collect, organize, and distribute food for benevolence
College ministry team	v. 40	Mail love packets, send e-encouragements
Benevolence teaching team	v. 36	Teach job training, GED, ESL, computer, sewing classes
Meals on Wheels ministry team	v. 35	Deliver meals along with Scripture, sermon tapes
Library outreach team	v. 35	Neighborhood story-time outreach
LIGHT Brigade team	v. 36	Accomplish one-hour tasks for homebound
Love crafts ministry team	v. 35	Make small gifts for ministry team use
Quill ministry team	v. 40	Write encouragement/prayer notes
Missionary pen pals team	v. 40	Write letters of encouragement
ICU hospital ministry team	v. 36	Visit waiting rooms; snack basket
Prayer walking plus ministry team	v. 35	Prayer walk and minister in different area weekly
E-outreach ministry team	v. 35	Use computer bank to send encouragements
School mentoring ministry team	v. 35	Lunch with assigned troubled children in public school
Servant ministry project team	v. 35	Perform unique ministry projects weekly

Tape ministry team	v. 40	Copy and mail sermon CDs for ministry
Christmas House benevolence ministry team	v. 35	Prepare toy shop for used and new toys for Christmas benevolence
Other ministry teams	vv. 35–36	Plenty of other options. Look around your community.

What Is a Ministry Team?

In our model program women have enjoyed a class, they've chatted over coffee, and now it's time for action: ministry teams. A ministry team is a group of at least two women who go into the community to minister to others in Jesus' name for one hour each week. Scripture challenges us with these words, "Set an example of good works yourself" (Titus 2:7). Ministry teams help women create that pattern.

Using specific parameters described in this chapter, you will provide several choices of well-planned, hands-on teams to fit the needs of your town and the gifts and interests of women in your church. Take a look at the ministry teams listed on the previous pages. Over past years each of the teams listed has been used in our model women's ministry. As you confer with the pastor and observe the local community, you'll discover great opportunity for ministry in Jesus' name. Pray for God's guidance, seek committed leaders, and offer as many ministry opportunities as possible.

There is a ministry team leader for each ministry, so if you have three ministry teams, you'll have three ministry team leaders. Thirteen teams, thirteen ministry team leaders. These are the most important leaders of the women's program. Each team leader works to become an expert in her ministry area, such as benevolence, hospital visits, or ministry to newcomers in town.

Quote from Survey (woman in her thirties)

"My favorite part of LIGHT is the ministry teams. I still can't believe someone plans out a ministry for me to do!"

Because leaders prepare well, it's astounding what can be accomplished in just an hour each week. When women arrive for ministry teams, every detail has been prepared. Most ministry teams will leave the church building almost immediately and will quickly be all over the community, ministering to others in Christ's name. All women have to do is show up and shine!

For example, a welcome wagon ministry team delivers welcome bags to new-comers in your town to invite them to your church. In preparation the leader has subscribed to a newcomer service to gather names of new move-ins. She gathers items for the welcome baskets or bags and prepares them. She maps visits geographi-cally for the teams. When women arrive for ministry, they are divided into twos, grab their assignments, and go. The nursing home ministry team leader, similarly, has established a relationship with the nursing home staff, makes specific assign-ments, and gathers needed materials. The ministry assignments are timed precisely to fit the one-hour time allotted.

The leadership team should say yes to as many teams as possible. If a woman is enthusiastic about leading a ministry team, others will join her. A few ministry teams may be dropped each semester because of leadership changes or disinterest. Other ministries should be added each semester. More teams allow more ministry. This stimulates interest and provides new opportunities for participants.

Each semester women may choose to sign up for a different ministry team, and they participate in that team for an entire fall or spring semester. Women are encouraged (but not forced) to select a different ministry each semester. A positive peer pressure ensures that ladies who come for the fellowship classes stay for the ministry hour. Amazingly, many who begin attending women's ministry for some-thing as simple as a scrapbooking class quickly learn that their greatest joy comes in ministering in Jesus' name!

For Him   Ministry Teams
Must Fit Matthew 25:35–36
For Others!
Hands-on
In the Name of the Lord

Parameters for a Ministry Team

How can you determine if a proposed group should occur during the fellowship class time or ministry teams? By creating specific parameters for ministry teams, you can assure that outward-focused hands-on ministry takes place during ministry hour.

> "Then the King will say to those on His right, 'Come, you who are blessed by My Father, inherit the kingdom prepared for you from the foundation of the world.
>
> For I was hungry and you gave Me something to eat;
>
> I was thirsty and you gave Me something to drink;
>
> I was a stranger and you took Me in;
>
> I was naked and you clothed Me;
>
> I was sick and you took care of Me;
>
> I was in prison and you visited Me.'
>
> "Then the righteous will answer Him, 'Lord, when did we see You hungry and feed You, or thirsty and give You something to drink? When did we see You a stranger and take You in, or without clothes and clothe You? When did we see You sick, or in prison, and visit You?'
>
> "And the King will answer them, 'I assure you: Whatever you did for one of the least of these brothers of Mine, you did for Me.'"
>
> (Matthew 25:34–40)

Take a closer look at these verses in Matthew. You'll be surprised at how many different ministries fit. The chart on pages 76–78 lists ministry teams used in the model women's ministry program.

In our program, the following four parameters were set for our ministry teams:

1. For others. Is it outward focused? This most often means they leave the building.

2. It is found in Matthew 25:35–36.

3. It is hands-on ministry—not studying or talking about the ministry but doing it.

4. It will be done in Jesus' name, not just with good deeds.

When a new potential ministry team is proposed, use the chart on page 82 to evaluate it. If it fits these parameters and can fit in the time frame, discuss it with the pastor or church liaison for approval. If any one of the parameters doesn't fit, it may still be offered during the fellowship class hour.

For example, a local school needed one-hour mentors for problem children. They allowed our women to wear their church name tags. The Meals on Wheels organization allowed our teams to wear church name tags and add Scriptures and sermon tapes to the meal trays. They fit the parameters.

Now you decide. Jean suggests a ministry team that will make quilts for the needy, and Andrea wants to teach a Spanish language class as a ministry team. Use the checklist to determine if these should be ministry teams or fellowship classes.

The quilt project fits almost all the parameters, but it is not a hands-on ministry to other people. Members would be staying at the church and quilting together, *preparing* for ministry. It would, however, be perfect for the fellowship class hour; and if they wanted to contribute a quilt to the hands-on benevolence ministry team, that would be great. The Spanish language class is an excellent suggestion, but because members are not physically *ministering to* others while they learn, it would fit the fellowship class hour. A good option, however, could be to offer the language class during the class hour and encourage attenders to join the benevolence team to practice their language skills. Got the picture?

Ministry Team or Fellowship Class Hour?

Use this chart to determine if an idea qualifies as a ministry team. If any box is unchecked, the idea may be offered during the fellowship class hour.

Proposed Ministry Team	Matthew 25 verse	Approved by pastor/ leadership team	For others	Done in Jesus' name	Hands-on	Fits time slot	Committed leader	Ministry Team or Fellowship Class?
Hospital visits	✓ v. 31	✓	✓	✓	✓	✓	✓	Ministry team
Quilting group								Fellowship class

Small Church Tip

Ministry teams work perfectly for a small church! Below is a list of some ministry teams that can begin with only two women each. Additional women can easily join and enhance the team's effectiveness. So a group of eight women could offer three or four different ministry teams. When newcomers arrive, they'll have lots of options. Suggested teams: nursing home, hospital, outreach, e-mail, e-outreach, homebound, missionary pen pals, new mommy ministry, prison Bible correspondence, or welcome ministry.

Very Small Church Tip

For a church with fewer than fifty in worship attendance, consider this option for ministry teams. From the survey, choose the four most requested ministries and schedule the entire group to do a different one together each meeting.

Ministry Team Overviews

A few summaries are provided below to help you understand ministry teams.

WELCOME MINISTRY TEAM

"I was a stranger, and you took Me in" (Matt. 25:35).

Members of the welcome team go in pairs to welcome new move-ins in the community, share Christ, and invite them to worship at your church. The team leader obtains names of newcomers from a service or from denominational resources. She prepares bags and maps, grouping visits geographically. The welcome bags contain a welcome letter from the pastor, church information, and a small gift. The gift may be a locally made product, such as hot sauce in San Antonio. It could be a handmade item. Our homebound members baked breads for gifts, and a ceramics group made personalized items. The love crafts team often made Scripture bookmarks or magnets with the church name. We once delivered a homemade pie to each new move-in in a nearby subdivision. The gifts may vary, but the thought is the same: "You are welcome. You are important. God loves you." After the visit, team members send a personal note to the newcomers. If your community is growing quickly, the team may need to stay at the church one week each month to mail welcome notes to newcomers they missed visiting.

CLOTHES CLOSET MINISTRY TEAM

"I was naked and you clothed Me" (Matt. 25:36).

The ministry team distributes donated used clothing for benevolence. The leader researches a benevolence ministry and prepares paperwork and witnessing brochures. The ladies on this team sort and organize, greet guests, do paperwork, distribute the clothing, and share Christ with those in the waiting area. A separate ministry may be added to assist needy women with appropriate clothing for job interviews.

FOOD PANTRY MINISTRY TEAM

"I was hungry and you gave Me something to eat" (Matt. 25:35).

This team organizes and staffs a food pantry to share with the needy in the community. Church members are invited to donate nonperishable food. The leader researches benevolence ministry, prepares paperwork and witnessing brochures. Team members sort and organize, greet guests, do paperwork, bag food, and share Christ. The team leader would benefit from a visit to an effective food and clothing pantry in a nearby city.

Quote from Survey (woman in her forties)

"My best friends in life are those I met while working together in the food pantry."

HOSPITAL MINISTRY TEAM

"I was sick and you took care of Me" (Matt. 25:36).

You won't believe this, but some folks in our church actually scheduled their hospitalization on women's ministry day! Teams of two or three visit the local hospital, seeing church members and friends who are there. They often take small gifts made by the love crafts team. The visits are brief and conclude with a prayer.

The hospital ministry team leader gathers a list of those who are in the hospital, ascertains that team members are aware of hospital rules, and pairs visitors in teams of two each week. On the first day of each semester, she gives a brief lesson about hospital etiquette. A sample handout is found on page 93. She has an alternate plan for days when there are no hospital patients, such as visiting a member with a long-term illness.

HOMEBOUND MINISTRY TEAM

"I was sick and you took care of Me" (Matt. 25:36).

The purpose of your homebound ministry is to visit church members who are unable to get out and be involved with other people. The visits provide conversation, spiritual encouragement, and practical help to an often forgotten segment of our society.

The team may visit homebound church members on a rotation basis, going in groups of two. They visit by appointment and may make one or two visits each week. They can take a church bulletin, sermon tape, or small gift prepared by the love craft ministry team.

The team leader gathers contact information for homebound members and friends, makes the appointments, prepares maps, and gathers materials. The visitors listen, laugh, chat about God's past and future blessings, and pray together before leaving.

Near their birthday, the team serves homebound members a birthday tea as a special treat, arriving with a basket containing china cups, a thermos of hot water, tea bags, and cookies.

Quote from Survey

"It's such a beautiful thing. . . . I visit our homebound, hoping they will receive a blessing. Instead, I receive the much greater blessing!"

LOVE CRAFTS MINISTRY TEAM

"Whatever you did for . . . the least of these . . ., you did for Me" (Matt. 25:40).

The strategy of ministry teams is to go out into the community. However, a few elderly women or nursing mothers in our group need to remain on campus. A creative leader helps this team create hundreds of handcrafted gifts for each of the other ministries to share with others. For example, they may decorate bags or baskets for the welcome ministry, sew lap quilts for the homebound, paint Scripture cards for Meals on Wheels or those in the hospital, or make wheelchair bags or outdoor wind socks for the nursing home team. They make magnets for outreach and personalized ceramic booties for the new mommies ministry. Many creations incorporate Scripture, and the team often uses recycled or excess donated items.

OUTREACH MINISTRY TEAM

"I was a stranger and you took Me in" (Matt. 25:35).

Ladies make personal visits to homes of people who have recently visited your church. They deliver a packet of information about the church, invite them to your church, and share God's plan of salvation. A separate team could make outreach telephone calls and mail and e-mail contacts.

NURSING HOME MINISTRY TEAM

"I was sick and you took care of Me" (Matt. 25:36).

Women visit a local nursing home to share a smile and God's love. This ministry may be approached in a variety of methods. Teams of two may visit an assigned hallway each week to chat, read the Bible, or write letters for residents. By visiting the same rooms each week, friendships develop.

Some nursing homes encourage a weekly class, such as a Bible study. One team of two women read the Bible aloud in the common area of a nursing home. By reading for thirty minutes each week, they completed the New Testament in one year. Another group played banana bingo weekly, closing with a short devotional. A different group of young women, who called themselves "door darlings," made seasonal door decorations and long-term relationships with residents.

A team of women could plan a monthly special event, rotating to visit four different nursing homes. This could be a hymn-sing musical team or a birthday party group with a port-a-party box of crepe paper, balloons, and birthday napkins. A special prayer may be offered for each honoree.

The story continues . . .

Be creative with your ministry. I went along one week to take a photograph of our manicure ministry team at the nursing home. They arrived, loaded with their little plastic totes of nail polish, to paint fingernails. The nursing home staff had set up a small table for each one, and a row of residents awaited them when they arrived weekly.

Trying to help out, I attempted to direct a lady from a long line to a shorter one. She exclaimed, "Oh, no, dear! I always go to Sandy."

As team members paint nails, they offer the ministry of touch. They listen with loving ears. They share Jesus. And each manicure ends with a prayer.

LIBRARY MINISTRY TEAM

"I was a stranger, and you invited me in" (Matt. 25:35).

Post an exterior sign and deliver invitations to neighbors to bring their children for a weekly story time in the church library. An animated storyteller entertains children with Bible stories while team members greet parents. Use puppets for added interest. This is a unique method of inviting strangers into your church, and children in GLO (God's Little Ones kids program) may be included.

QUILL MINISTRY TEAM

"I was a stranger, and you invited me in" (Matt. 25:35).

This industrious team writes notes to recent church visitors, college students, local and national leaders, neighbors who lived near the church, military personnel, missionaries, people mentioned in the local newspaper who need prayer, policemen, firemen, bereaved, sick, homebound, and inactive church members. They could send an encouragement note to every Sunday school teacher.

One semester we titled this team "missionary pen pals," and team members wrote to several missionaries supported by our church. Our quill ministry team was primarily composed of women who needed to stay at the church building, such as nursing mothers and some elderly members.

Because a handwritten note is a rare commodity in today's world, recipients treasure them. The leader prepares a poster with sample notes and Scriptures to get them started. Ask women's ministry members to contribute excess stationery from home or purchase sale paper for this ministry.

LIGHT BRIGADE MINISTRY TEAM

"I was sick and you visited me" (Matt. 25:36).

The LIGHT Brigade schedules and performs one task for those in need of help because of long-term illness or age. Our LIGHT Brigade team had a specific list of jobs they could accomplish, such as planting flowers, painting a front door or small room, changing lightbulbs and smoke alarm batteries, or cleaning a freezer, pantry, or windows. The team leader scheduled projects and ascertained that supplies were available, and each team took an extra person to visit with the homebound person.

Selecting Ministry Teams

How do you determine which ministry teams to offer? Begin with ministries within your church that are already functioning and would like assistance. For example, two women in our church visited a nearby nursing home regularly. When we inquired about their willingness to train and plan for others to assist them, they were ecstatic. They not only had the initial contacts in place at the nursing home; they also had a love for that ministry and experience and ideas to share.

Select ministry teams to fit your church goals, the passion and interest of potential ministry team leaders, and the needs in your church field. Confer with your pastor and church leaders. They may be aware of great needs in your community. Is there a need for help with a homeless ministry? Is there a prison or hospital near your church? Can you see a need for a welcome team for a new subdivision nearby? Your church building is surrounded by people who desperately need to meet Jesus Christ. Look around and discover how your women's group can meet needs.

The story continues . . .

If someone has a new idea for a ministry team, consider it carefully. If it fits the required parameters, say yes!

One spring a talented and godly artist in our church approached our ministry coordinator with an idea for a new ministry team. She wanted to offer art classes as therapy for victims of stroke. She would read Scripture, play Christian music while they painted, and help stroke victims in our community to regain some of the use of their hands by teaching them paint brush strokes. This definitely fit our Scripture, "I was sick and you took care of Me"!

She advertised the class, recruited an assistant to help, and the two of them made a difference in the lives of three people in our community that we would have otherwise never touched. One of those came to know Jesus as her Savior and became an active member of our church.

Our leadership team would never in a million years have thought of an art therapy ministry team, but God put this idea in the heart of one of His servants. Though it was only offered one semester, it was a point of LIGHT.

Offer as many different ministry team choices as possible. You will find that each well-planned ministry opportunity will attract different ladies. Many ministries, such as a hospital team, function well with just two or three participants, and they will make a significant impact in ministry.

Schedule an entire year of ministry teams at a time, and pay careful attention to needs and opportunities for next year's ministry teams. Some teams may only function for one semester because of needs or leadership interest, but that's not a problem. It helps keep women's ministry fresh. Add at least one new ministry team each semester.

Quote from Survey

"Every time I leave LIGHT, I know I've accomplished something worthwhile in Jesus' name."

Perfect Preparation

Each ministry team leader makes careful preparation, so participants just show up and "shine!" The hospital team leader, for example, will establish contact and needed permissions from the local hospitals, gather names of members and friends who are hospitalized, prepare maps or gifts, and plan any needed training for ministry team members. She may prepare a handout similar to the one on page 93. If hospital locations are difficult, she may have a notebook with maps for each team. Careful preparation expands ministry potential.

High Priority

Christians are instructed to "be rich in good works" (1 Tim. 6:18). In our model women's ministry, a constant effort was exerted to keep ministry as a priority. In promotional materials the ministry teams were more prominently displayed than events or classes. Leaders in every area of women's ministry were encouraged to set an example of involvement in a ministry team.

At the kickoff event, displays or visuals for ministry teams were intentionally given a more visible role or placement than other areas of the program.

Sample Business Card

L.I.G.H.T.
Ladies Intentionally
Going, Helping, Touching
A Ministry of the **Fresh Ideas Church**

You Have Been Ministered To By:

_____

www.KeepOnShining.com

Quote from Survey

"A lady I welcomed to our community through the welcome ministry team is now a new Christian, a member of our church, and my best friend."

Tips for the Ministry Team Coordinator

Tips for assisting, training, and encouraging ministry team leaders.

Assist

- Accompany a different ministry team each week.
- Provide business cards, sample above, with the women's ministry logo, church name, and Web site.
- Provide organizational tips and tools.
- Help the team leader with descriptive words for the semester's brochure.
- Help recruit team participants for each ministry.
- Assist team leaders with their presentation for the kickoff. A capable ministry team leader may not have creative ideas for a display table or costume.
- Provide laminated wall signs for each ministry team. Hang them high on the walls at the coffee break area for easy assembly and exit for ministry.
- Attempt to provide resources needed. In our model women's ministry, each ministry team received a token budget amount each semester. It was amazing to see how it stretched.

Train

- Connect team leaders with similar leaders in other churches in your area. For example, the food pantry team leader may enjoy visiting other food ministries to help with planning.
- Inform leaders about training and resources available through national, state, and local denominational resources.
- Be alert for ideas and resources from current books, magazines, and online sites.

Encourage

- Take an action photo of each group every semester. Use them for a pre-luncheon slide show, hallway television monitors, or historical scrapbook.
- Brag about successes of ministry teams.
- Take each team leader to lunch occasionally. Listen. Applaud. Pray.
- Send occasional e-mail notes to encourage and update ministry team leaders.

Tips for Ministry Team Leaders

- *Become an expert on your ministry topic.* Visit your local Christian bookstore and church library to find books full of suggestions for most ministry groups. Attend national, state, and associational training events to enhance your knowledge. Research. Network with leaders of similar ministries in other churches for ideas.

- *Be committed.* Make a commitment to lead this ministry team for a minimum of one year. Arrive early. Recruit an assistant to help you and substitute if needed. Set an example in faithful church attendance and Christian living. Attend any required meetings.

- *Get organized.* When your team members arrive, their responsibility is to carry out the ministry, not to talk about it or prepare for it. Take care of all details. Keep a separate bag for resource materials and a notebook of team members' contact information, ministry data, and ministry records. Most ministries will require approximately two hours of outside preparation time.

- *Be enthusiastic.* Make it fun. Learn your team members' names. Pray for them. Check on them if they're absent.

- *Encourage fellowship.* Most ministry teams go out in twos, so rearrange pairs occasionally. Invite an individual team member for lunch, or meet as a team after ministry time. Know the spiritual condition of team members, and personally share Christ with any who are not Christians. Pay special attention to help newcomers make friends. Make a follow-up call to first-time guests.

- *Accept suggestions and criticism with joy.* Brainstorm with team members to develop the best possible ministry plans. Curtail gossip.

- *Get out of there!* Begin right on time. Pray with team members before sending them off. Plan how to include newcomers. Plan ministry to fit within the scheduled hour. The goal is for every ministry team to be out the door and into the community within five minutes.

- *Never forget your primary purpose:* to share Jesus with others.

Tips for Making a Hospital Visit

Before the Visit

- Be faithful and enthusiastic about this ministry opportunity.

- Before you leave your car, pray with your visitation partner for God's blessings on your visits today. Pray for His direction, wisdom, and joy.

- Wear your church name tag. It will make the patient feel more comfortable.

- Do not chew gum or wear perfume.

- Wash your hands before visiting and between visits. There is more danger of passing germs to patients than in getting germs from them.

During the Visit

- If there is a notice on the door, obey it. If visitors are not allowed, leave a note with the nurse.

- Knock softly, wait for an answer, and then enter. As you enter, observe details. For example, notice the presence or absence of cards, flowers, and visitors. Ask God, "How can you use me to share your love to this patient?"

- Place yourself sitting or standing in direct line of vision of the person in order to maximize opportunity for speaking and listening without strain. Never sit, lean on, or touch the bed. Be polite and stand if there are not enough chairs. You're only going to be there a short time.

- Smile. Be relaxed and cheerful. Look confident and emanate the Lord's faith in the situation. Talk audibly. Don't yell. Don't whisper.

- When greeting the patient, introduce yourself by name as well as the name of your church. Call the patient by name. Tell why you have come. Let the conversation begin on a topic that is neutral.

- Never hug. When you pray for the patient, it may be appropriate to touch his or her arm or hand.

- Listen more than you talk. Sincerely care, but don't intrude. Unless you are a medical professional, never give medical advice. Do not share stories of your own medical history. Do not discuss others who have had a particular illness. Don't argue or contradict. Your task is to be supportive. Never express negative feelings while you are in the patient's room. Do not bear bad news.

- Do not eat the patient's food, either from his tray or from the gifts others have left.

- Ask, "Would you mind if I pray for you before I leave?" Offer a prayer of gratitude and trust. Don't make it too long or too specific.

- Share Scripture. Carry a small Bible marked with your favorite comforting Scripture. Before you pray, read an appropriate Scripture. Write it on a card and leave it for the patient to meditate on later.

- Leave something. Take the church bulletin or newsletter. If you enjoy crafts, make Scripture bookmarks. Take a flower from your garden, a card, or any small token that will remind the patient of your visit and of God's love.

- Most hospital visits last only a few minutes. Use common sense. The patients are in the hospital because they are sick, so be sensitive to the patient's energy and condition. Don't act rushed. The most important thing in the world you have to do is be with the person *right now*.

After the Visit

- As you leave the hospital, stop by the restroom and wash your hands.

- Send an e-mail or leave a phone message at the church office to inform the pastor of your visit and the patient's condition.

- Never discuss a patient's personal information with others.

- If there is a specific need, do your best to assist. If you promise to do something, do it.

- Continue to pray for the patient.

- Drop a note to remind the patient you're praying.

What If . . . ?

What if the patient is asleep? Let the patient sleep. Leave a card indicating that you were there.

What if relatives are there? Make a brief visit. Include the relative in your time of prayer. Call the relative by name.

What if the patient has a roommate? After greeting your patient, introduce yourself to the roommate. If the roommate feels like entering into the conversation, be sensitive to God's leading. He may have sent you to share Christ with the roommate! Include the roommate in the prayer.

What if the nurse or doctor comes in? Be polite and leave the room while medical personnel are attending the patient.

What if the patient wants to go for a walk? Check with the nurse first.

What if there is significant information I feel the church needs to know? Call the church office immediately.

CHAPTER 10

Fellowship Classes

Teaching is a light.

—**Proverbs 6:23**

Ladies love classes! I am constantly amazed at the response of women to fellowship classes. In our model women's ministry program, the first hour of the weekly schedule offers a choice of fun, purposeful classes. This hour is "all about me!" Ladies are given a choice of enticing classes, such as a topical Bible class, missions class, or a new crafts class.

You can call them fellowship classes, enLIGHTening classes, or growth classes; but the purpose is the same: personal and spiritual growth for women and Christian fellowship. Though it's only a portion of the program, it's a strategic part.

Stats from Survey

On a scale of one to ten, 95 percent of our women rated their fellowship class a ten. One hundred percent said their class was well planned and worth attending. Ninety percent said they made new friends.

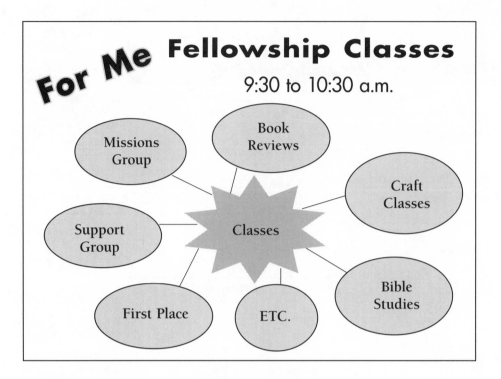

It's a Hook

Classes will attract newcomers to your women's ministry. A weight-loss Bible study or scrapbooking class might entice women to attend who've never been to church. Church members who have never engaged in women's ministry may register enthusiastically for a semester of parenting Bible studies or an aerobics class. Each different class, whether it is for personal or spiritual growth, will appeal to different women. Regular attenders will invite friends to a new class. Once newcomers attend, they'll catch the excitement of Christian fellowship and the joy of the ministry teams.

When a woman who's never been in church joins your knitting class or missions study group or Bible study about finances, she'll notice something right away. There's joy in the room. The women have a confidence in their God that is hard for a lost person to comprehend. And they love one another. She probably expected the class to begin with prayer, but she certainly didn't expect *this*. Pure Christian fellowship is an attractive thing.

She'll find friends. She'll do lunch with the girls. They'll talk about how Jesus impacts their lives. There's an energy that's enticing, and the longer she hangs around, the more she learns of God. And *you* may be the one who gets to lead her to salvation!

Quote from Survey

"In two years of LIGHT, I've learned to make crazy quilts and stained glass, how to lose weight biblically, and how to balance my checkbook. More important, I learned how to pray with a sick person in the hospital, and I've discovered the value of Christian friendship."

A Variety of Classes

Variety adds spice. An assortment of quality classes will attract a variety of women. Attendance will increase as you increase choices. Our model women's ministry offers classes in three categories: Bible, crafts/special interest, and missions classes. Each category is discussed in this chapter.

Some classes last an entire fall or spring semester, and others last half of a semester. This plan creates a mid-semester entry point for newcomers. Women are free to join a different class each time.

The fellowship class ideas chart on pages 100–101 lists several classes that our women's ministry offered over the past several years. Don't be limited to these ideas, though. Get current. Do something that interests women in your church today.

Attempt to offer at least two choices of fellowship classes in a small church and more in a larger church. Though popular classes may be repeated a second semester, we rarely found it successful. If the schedule includes repeated classes, be sure you have plenty of new classes also.

Quote from Survey

"Our fellowship classes are great—lots of variety for spiritual, physical, social, and creative needs. I love it."

Class Size

Yes, multiple classes will increase interest and attendance, but use good judgment when determining the number of classes to offer. For example, if you have a possibility of twenty ladies to attend your women's ministry, it may be wise to offer three class choices instead of six. (Six ministry teams would work, however!)

Some classes may be large; others will be small. No class should be "full," especially for newcomers. You may print a recommended maximum number on some classes, but don't turn away a woman who would like to sign up for a class. Do not attempt to make all the class sizes the same, leveling registration and limiting class size. Encourage women to choose the classes they would most enjoy.

An ideal number for many classes is four to nine women, allowing personalized teaching, class participation, and relationship-building. Our leadership team members sometimes participated in smaller classes to help with class size.

Fellowship Class Ideas

- Bible study class
  - Heaven
  - Marriage
  - Ephesians
  - Parenting
  - MasterLife
  - Witnessing
  - How to pray
  - Spiritual gifts
  - Experiencing God
  - Christian finance
  - Angels, with craft
  - Women in the Bible
  - First Place Bible study
  - Video Bible class,
  - Beth Moore/Ann Graham Lotz
  - More at Lifeway.com or Newhopepublishers.com
- Women on Mission
- Mission book study
- Grandparents rearing grandkids
- Birthday party planning
- Christian book reviews

- Parenting, age groups
- Window treatments
- Family traditions
- Spanish language
- Support groups
- Sign language
- Meal planning
- Self-defense
- Entertaining
- Aerobics
- First aid
- Cooking
- One-day crafts series
- Painting techniques
- Porcelain doll faces
- Plastic canvas art
- Christmas crafts
- Rubber stamping
- Scherenschnitte
- Cake decorating
- Wreath making

- T-shirt making
- Basket making
- Gift-wrapping
- Wallpapering
- Stained glass
- Scrapbooking
- Gifts for kids
- Cotton press
- Floral design
- Tole painting
- Crazy quilts
- Embroidery

- Watercolor
- First Place
- Calligraphy
- Stenciling
- Smocking
- Parenting
- Ceramics
- Crochet
- Knitting
- Quilting
- Sewing
- Collars

Requirements for All Class Leaders

- Christian, committed member of our church
- Faithfully involved in Sunday school and worship
- Approved through proper church processes (Bible teachers)
- Participates in a ministry team as an example to her students
- Prepares her class to the best of her ability "as unto the Lord!"

Where Do We Find Teachers?

Potential teachers will surface with the annual church survey and year-end evaluation forms. Ask the pastor and ministry staff of your church for suggestions. Ask adult Sunday school teachers if a member of their class might be a potential leader. Strictly follow biblical parameters and guidelines set by your church regarding Bible teachers. Keep a notebook of potential leaders.

Because classes are a short-term commitment, you may discover more potential teachers than you expected. Any class leader for your women's ministry should be a faithful, supportive member of your church.

In addition to planning a variety of different classes, involve a variety of class leaders. For example, when you look at your one-year program, the same woman should not lead every Bible study. She may lead one semester, skip a semester, and then lead another. Having a variety of classes and class leaders allows more women to use their gifts to serve God, creates anticipation and movement, and helps avoid a "sameness" mentality. You'll be amazed at how God will provide just the right Bible teachers and class leaders.

Bible Classes

Bible study changes lives, and the possibilities for Bible class topics are vast. Choose Bible study curriculum carefully, ascertaining that the study reflects the doctrines and beliefs of your church. Bible study materials will need to be approved through your church. The approval process may be simplified if your church denomination has a publishing arm, such as Southern Baptists' LifeWay Christian Resources.

Pray for God's guidance for class selections. Carefully study suggestions from the all-church survey and year-end evaluations to discover needs.

Tips for Class Leaders

- Before the first class, call each person on your registration list to tell her you're looking forward to seeing her there.
- Arrive early. Pray for your class members before they arrive. Write something interesting on the board. Display visuals. Visit with early arrivers.
- On the first day share your personal Christian testimony.
- Begin and end exactly on time every week. Set the pace on day one.
- Prepare your class so well that it's worth each woman's morning! Vary teaching methods. Encourage interaction. Use handouts. Rearrange the classroom occasionally.
- If you are leading a video Bible study, carefully select the portions of the video you will project.
- Invite everyone you know to attend your class.
- Help class members meet new friends. Invite the class to meet for lunch one day.
- Call ladies by name. Speak to them at church. Check on them if they miss class.

- Know the spiritual condition of class members. If a woman doesn't attend church, invite her. Introduce her to Christ.

- Squelch gossip. Conduct your class with integrity and redirect negative talk. Read Titus 2:3–5 before you teach each class.

- Never call on a woman to lead prayer or read aloud unless you have asked her in advance.

- Include newcomers in discussion without putting them on the spot.

- Whether you're teaching Revelation or knitting, your class should point toward God. If you're leading a craft class, chat about how God impacts your daily life. Always begin class with Scripture or prayer.

- Take part in a ministry team. Set an example of faithful support and participation at your church.

- Recruit an assistant teacher to substitute in an emergency.

- Dismiss your class promptly. Turn out the classroom light and enjoy the fellowship coffee, returning later for cleanup.

"Whatever you do, do it enthusiastically,
as something done for the Lord and not for men" (Col. 3:23).

BIBLE TOPICS

Ask your pastor or staff liaison for suggestions. Pay attention to needs around you. Walk through the Christian bookstore. Shop online for ideas at lifeway.com. If you have a specific Bible teacher in mind, ask if she has a study or topic she would enjoy teaching. Contact your denomination's state or local office for recommendations, resources, and contact information for other women's ministry leaders around your state. Keep a notebook of suggested Bible topics for future semesters.

If your women's ministry will offer more than one Bible study each semester, consider choosing one with homework and one without. Those variations appeal to totally different women. Topical studies were often the favorite choices with our group. If one Bible study is targeted toward preschool mothers or widows, select the second study for a more generic appeal.

Quote from Survey

"I've grown as a new Christian, and I've had such fun ministering to others."

When selecting classes, choose studies that can fit the allotted time. Occasionally we would offer a ninety-minute class, such as a video Bible class or watercolor class, and invite participants to arrive earlier for that class. Since child care would not be open, mothers would make other arrangements or take their children when child care began. Most often, however, those leading a video class would elect to review the video to preselect portions to play during class and personally teach most of the class.

What if the predesigned number of class sessions for a study doesn't fit the allotted weeks exactly? For example, the class about spiritual gifts is designed for a six-week session, but this semester's session is seven weeks long. A teacher may add an introductory session, allowing volunteers to share their testimony and get to know one another. Alternately, she may combine classes to shorten the time frame.

Some classes, such as *Experiencing God, First Place,* or a Beth Moore Bible study, will last the entire fall or spring semester—twelve to fifteen weeks. Other choices, such as Christmas wreath-making or a *Jesus on Money* class, may last a half semester of six to eight sessions.

A combination of semester-long and half-semester classes is most desirable. Some women will gladly commit for a shorter study, and those half-semester classes provide an easy entry point at midterm for newcomers. Remember the rule: choices increase attendance.

Most important, teach the Bible. Never offer a Bible study class where most of the time is spent chatting about community events or husbands or kids. Get into God's Word.

The story continues . . .

On our year-end evaluation forms, several ladies requested a Bible study about Christian finances. Larry Burkett had just released a wonderful six-week Bible study, but we wanted a woman who was financially and spiritually qualified to lead it.

I stood in the children's hallway at church, chatting with a young mother named Kathy. A work-at-home mom, she was telling me about how God had provided for her family. In conversation she mentioned that her college degree was in finance. Here stood an answer to prayer: an active church member, a godly mother and wife, and a CPA. Wow!

Kathy led that Bible class about finances with care and wisdom, and many new mothers attended just to hear her teach. They were blessed. She was blessed. God was honored.

CRAFTS AND SPECIAL INTEREST CLASSES

Crafts and special interest classes can be as varied as the talents and interests of ladies in your church. Because the classes change every semester, stagnation will not occur. An ever-changing assortment of interesting classes keeps your women's ministry fresh.

Though the classes in this category may not appear "religious," the leader is a committed Christian and a positive member of your church. She may begin class with prayer and a Scripture or testimony. She will guide classroom discussion to honor God. She will minister to class participants, pray for them, and help them make Christian friends. She will attempt to make every word—even about crochet!—honor God.

As newcomers attend the class and enjoy the large-group coffee and fellowship, they'll also be enticed to become involved in the ministry hour. They will have the opportunity to choose a different class each semester, perhaps a Bible study. They will receive multiple invitations to worship on Sunday if they don't attend church somewhere. Women in the group will intentionally share Jesus with them. And women's ministry will happen.

The possibilities are almost limitless. How do you determine a good variety of classes to offer each semester? Begin by carefully reviewing the survey forms from your all-church survey to discover interests and talents. Read magazines or walk through the craft store. Your problem will not be finding good possibilities for classes; it will be deciding which classes to offer this semester! To be honest, our Bible and missions classes had larger attendances than the crafts classes most semesters, but craft classes provide a valuable option.

Work diligently to plan top-quality classes. Keep a notebook of ideas for future classes and leaders. As you discover potential topics and leaders, future planning will be simplified. After your women's ministry gets going, you may often schedule classes a year ahead of time. For example, when we learned that Rose could teach a stained glass class, it was penciled in for the spring semester a year later. It created great anticipation! If a woman knows that she's teaching a knitting class next fall, she will likely be involved before that time.

Don't limit classes to crafts. Over the years we had a wide array of interesting classes, such as support groups, low-impact aerobics, cooking, and self-defense.

When ladies register for classes, they pay for their workbooks, books, or craft supplies. If a craft leader prefers that class members purchase their own supplies, a detailed list is provided at registration. Some fees may be optional, such as the *Missions Mosaic* magazine for the missions class. Always offer at least one class choice with no monetary cost involved. Provide an inconspicuous method of providing scholarships for those with need. Our church budget paid for leaders' teaching books.

We never allowed classes for fund-raising, and no instructor could lead a class that would benefit her economically. It's easy to find instructors for classes who are selling products, but that changes the entire atmosphere and purpose. Set a hard and fast rule, and it may save many headaches.

Some classes may naturally feed into a specific ministry team. For example, a *Share Jesus without Fear* witnessing class could practice what they learned by participating in the outreach ministry team.

Stats from Survey

Someone recently commented, "Younger adults these days just don't care about missions." That's a myth! Thirty women under the age of forty completed our year-end survey, and 100 percent of them indicated, "I love our emphasis on missions."

MISSIONS CLASS

Why add a missions class? If your focus is upward and outward, a consistent missions education and missions support group is a great asset to your class schedule. Prepare a quality program to enhance missions awareness about missionaries supported by your church.

For example, our Southern Baptist church used the excellent materials provided by Women on Mission (www.wmu.com). The informative weekly program features a variety of teaching techniques and projects. Since the denomination has more than ten thousand foreign and domestic missionaries, there is plenty to learn! WMU will assist with training and organizing the class.

Our Women on Mission group was in existence before we began the combined women's ministry, and they were instrumental in encouraging the larger organization. Interestingly, after the women's ministry program began, our Women on Mission group grew consistently larger than ever in its history. Women of all ages would select the missions class for a semester, and the total number of women learning about missions multiplied.

Every woman in our ministry group was impacted by our missions group. They felt informed and involved in missions.

Missions, Missions, Everywhere!

A missionary focus permeates our entire women's ministry group with large and small doses of missions information and encouragement sprinkled throughout. Some examples:

- A table near the registration area displays current missionary newsletters and denominational missions materials.

- Prayer assignments for missionaries are given to every attender each week. A member of our Women on Mission group designs clever note cards, magnets, or bookmarks with the name of an SBC missionary with a birthday that day. As ladies leave for their ministry teams, each receives a different missionary's name and prays for that missionary during the week. They take their assignments seriously. (When I visited friends' homes, I would often notice their missionary prayer assignment on the refrigerator or bulletin board.)

- The International Mission Board (www.imb.org) and North American Mission Board (www.namb.net) produce fabulous video clips. Show them on video monitors at registration or luncheon gathering area.

- Provide refrigerator magnets with prayer line numbers for missionaries. NAMB 1-800-554-PRAY and IMB 1-800-395-PRAY.

- Encourage women to subscribe to *Missions Mosaic* magazine. You can order copies from Woman's Missionary Union, www.wmu.com.

- When the missions class has a missionary speaker, invite all members to meet for lunch to chat with him or her.

- Introduce guest missionaries during coffee break and pray for them.
- Plan group projects to assist a missionary with a specific need.
- When mission trips are planned for your church, your women's ministry group may help with prayer support, materials preparation, or gift packages for missionaries.
- Support special weeks of prayer for missions.

The story continues . . .

It was unbelievable! In our small church, dozens of women showed up for the new women's ministry program. Small, struggling pieces of women's ministry were still in place, along with several new ones. The new emphasis on hands-on ministry created purpose, and our community was impacted. Women grew spiritually and made Christian friends. And our church's growth was positively affected.

We now had a women's ministry with a capital M!

"Too many choices!" That may be the biggest complaint about your new women's ministry. Today's women demand relevant, worthwhile activity; and when you offer a choice of classes, many individual needs may be met.

Just think about it. A Bible class about communication in marriage may be attended by only a few women, but those well may be women who have never come before. Does it sound like too much to offer five ministry teams in a small church? Definitely not! It only takes a couple of women to create an effective hospital team, nursing home team, outreach, or welcome ministry team. And by offering several teams, you're much more likely to attract other new attenders.

When a woman attends women's ministry for a specific class or ministry team, she'll reap the benefits of the rest of the morning's program, including the excitement of new prayer partners and friends and church involvement. All the pieces work together to create a vibrant overall program. Many women in your church and community are just waiting for something worthwhile. This is it.

You'll be amazed at how many women will show up when they're given choices of classes and ministries. So ease up a little, say yes when you possibly can, and allow several groups to function at the same time. Women love choices.

Small Church Tip

You may not be able to offer a dozen classes, but do something fresh.

Try this plan. Schedule a year's plan of combination fellowship classes. Each hour-long class will consist of a half-hour Bible class, a twenty-minute "just for fun" feature, and a ten-minute missions emphasis.

For example, one six-week class begins with a Bible study based on *The Frazzled Female* by Cindi Wood. A creative leader plans six short craft activities for the sessions, focusing on Christmas gifts to make or tips to make the Christmas season less frazzled. The missions feature focuses on missionaries in countries with "unfrazzled" lifestyles. Or how about a Bible study about angels, an angel craft, and missions stories about missionaries in difficult fields? Get creative with your one-year plan, include new people in leadership, and create new enthusiasm for loving and serving our great God.

After the combo fellowship class hour, ladies divide into teams of two for ministry teams such as hospital, homebound, and Welcome Wagon.

Small Church Sample Schedule of Ministries and Classes

Ministry Teams Spring Semester January 16–May 3 Thursdays, 10:45 a.m. Select one per semester.	Nursing Home Team	Prison Bible Correspondence Team	Welcome Ministry Team	Hospital/Homebound Ministry Team
	Visit, read, listen, and share God's love with residents.	Evaluate Bible studies; write encouraging notes to inmates.	Deliver welcome basket and church invitation to newcomers in our town.	Share joy and a visit with members who are sick.

Fellowship Classes Session 1 January 16–March 8 Thursdays, 9:30 a.m. Choose one.	Crazy Quilts	He Speaks to Me	Women on Missions
	Learn dozens of stitches and create a treasure!	Join this Bible study about preparing to hear from God, written by Priscilla Schirer.	Learn about missions in our world today.
Fellowship Classes Session 2 March 22–May 3 Thursdays, 9:30 a.m. Choose one.	Women on Mission	Purposeful Scrapbooking	Acts 1:8 Challenge
	Bible study, projects, and missionary encouragement and study.	An expert teaches a lovely way to journal God's blessings.	This Bible study by Nate Adams has a life-changing challenge.

Medium/Large Church Sample Schedule of Ministries and Classes
LIGHT Ministry Teams

Nursing Home
Visit church members and others in nursing homes to share God's love.

Welcome Wagon
Welcome new residents to our town, and introduce them to TBC with a smile, home baked goods, and a prayer.

New Mom Ministry
Deliver encouragement and Christian parenting materials to new moms.

Quill Ministry Team
Share God's love by writing and sending notes and letters to those who need encouragement.

Love Crafts Team
Those unable to go out can create handcrafted items for our ministry teams to share.

Library Ministry
We'll invite parents and preschoolers in our town to our church library for Bible stories.

Hospital Team
Visit local hospitals to encourage and share God's Word with those in our church and community who have health problems.

Homebound Team
Visit shut-ins to share God's love and provide practical help for community members who are unable to get out and be involved with other people.

Friendship House
Distribute tangible goods and God's love to the needy through food pantry and clothes closet.

Outreach
Make personal visits, telephone calls, and mail contacts to show that our church cares for those who recently visited our church.

Luncheons

March 15, 11:45 a.m. • "Love for More Than a Lifetime"
Speaker: Gena Sharp • Music: Joy Hanover
Mini-Feature: Wedding gown style show presented by women of Third Baptist Church

May 3, 11:45 a.m. • "Legacies of Life"
Speaker: Mary Cochran • Music: Carol Thompson
Mini-Feature: Children's fashion show
Special decor: Worldwide doll collection by Jan Smith

Medium/Large Church Sample Semester of Fellowship Classes

Third Quarter, January 26–March 8, 9:30 to 10:30 a.m. Thursdays (Choose one.)

Scrapbook Class	Ceramics	Sewing Tips	Once Upon A Time	A Heart Like His
An expert teaches how to scrapbook, emphasizing Christian legacy.	Enjoy our new kiln in this class for beginners who would like to create but think they have no talent.	Designed for moms and grandmas. Begin with laying patterns and learn to alter, repair, or make costumes.	Spiritual growth through Christian book reviews shared by a master story-teller.	A study of David reveals God's love in this Beth Moore Bible class (both sessions). (Workbook $13)
Women On Mission	**First Place Weight/Bible**	**Share Jesus without Fear**	**Conversation Peace**	**Aerobics**
Move from a milk-fed to a meat-fed Christian through prayer, Bible, and mission studies.	Learn to lose and keep off pounds with the Bible as your guide (both sessions). Prerequisite meeting January 4, 3:00 p.m., chapel.	Experience in-depth evangelism training and visitation the second hour.	Revolutionize speech habits with this Mary Kassian Bible class. (Workbook $10)	Exercise to Christian music and have time to get dressed for coffee and ministry teams. (Note: Aerobics will be from 9:00 to 10:00 a.m.)

Fourth Quarter, March 22-May 3, 9:30-10:30 Thursdays Choose one.

How Much Is Enough?	Women on Mission	Beginning Quilting	Parenting a Preschooler	Made It Myself!
Learn biblical truths related to finances in this Larry Burkett Bible study.	Learn to encourage missionaries and enjoy Bible study and fellowship with friends.	Make a lap rag quilt and learn the basics of a great craft.	Learn tips from God's Word about teaching, discipline, and loving your child.	Make a unique craft weekly for birthdays, weddings, and teacher gifts.
Stained Glass	Heart's Cry	Cooking In A Minute	First Place Weight/ Bible	A Heart Like His
This class for beginners includes design and basic stained glass.	Discover the principles of heart-changing prayer.	Have fun cooking with a bonus of mini-devotionals.	(Continued from first session.)	(Continued from first session.)

Make an eternal difference. LIGHT your world.

CHAPTER 11

Child Care

Let the little children come to Me.
— Jesus, Mark 10:14

I know. I know. Providing quality child care during your women's ministry is difficult, expensive, and inconvenient. If you want to include mothers of preschoolers in your women's ministry program, however, quality child care is an absolute necessity.

Study current materials and church policies regarding curriculum, security, scheduling, and staff training. Before beginning a women's ministry program, it may be necessary to schedule a workday for cleaning, painting, or updating the child-care facilities. It's worth the effort! Children will be taught about God's love, and mothers will attend if their children are happy.

Here are a few tips about child care during a women's ministry:

Name It

We called our kids program GLO, an acronym for "God's Little Ones," to go along with LIGHT.

Add Christian Teaching

What an opportunity to share Jesus with precious little ones! Mere babysitting is insufficient. Mothers will appreciate a plan to challenge and enrich their children spiritually. Incorporate a Bible curriculum for preschoolers, and post the day's Bible story title and memory verse for moms to see.

Fun Schedule

With over two hours to fill, the schedule can include snacks, outdoor and indoor playtime, Christian music, group games, library story time, Bible activities, or crafts. Print a schedule of activities and post it for moms to view.

GLO Visor

One semester we ordered inexpensive, brightly colored, GLO T-shirts for pre-schoolers. Moms purchased them, and kids loved wearing them on women's ministry days. Another semester we provided GLO visors. Get creative. Make it special.

One Unique Detail

Make an extra effort to plan a special weekly feature at GLO that children would not find at other times they attend church. For example, we asked a retired librarian in our church to plan an animated Bible story time for children. On luncheon days children brought sack lunches for a picnic. When several moms of older homeschool children attended women's ministry, those teens did a Bible study together, wrote a script, and performed a weekly puppet show for preschoolers.

No Recruits

It is rarely appropriate to ask women attending your women's ministry to rotate shifts to care for children. Not everyone is qualified or interested in caring for children, and begging for nursery volunteers may diminish attendance. Second, it rarely works. If someone in your church has a desire to assist with child care, thank God for them, and treat them like royalty, but don't harass others to work in the nursery.

Though it will take extra work and expense, make the effort to find qualified workers outside your church. Consider asking other churches in your area for recommendations. Are there college students in your church who could use extra income?

The expense of hiring qualified, caring workers to assist with those precious children is well worthwhile. Some women's ministries charge a nominal fee for each child. In our model women's ministry program, the vast majority of budget money was spent for child care, and God provided consistent, enthusiastic, godly workers.

Small Church Tip

Don't think that child care is exclusively a small church problem. Larger churches just have to find more workers! It may help with planning to ask mothers to make child-care reservations. Be flexible, of course, but ask moms to make a standing reservation, or they can call by a deadline for a one-time child-care reservation.

CHAPTER 12

Group Projects

A cord of three strands is not easily broken.
—Ecclesiastes 4:12

Group projects add interest and ministry impact to an already great program. They take little time from the scheduled program and are relatively simple to accomplish. They also provide short-term opportunities to involve new women in leadership. In our model women's program, at least one group project was planned each semester.

Just to get your thinking wheels turning, look at the chart of some group projects used in our model women's ministry on pages 120-121. A group project can be anything from collecting socks for the needy to a church cookbook project. Brainstorm potential projects at officers' meetings. Consult with your pastor for ideas. Ask a missionary how you can assist. Be ready to address community crises. Look around. You'll quickly have more ideas than you can use. Vary the projects each semester, and avoid consistent monetary demands. Most important, projects must fit your own church's mission statement and needs in your own community.

Group projects may sometimes tie in with church events projects. For example, if your church is sending a mission team overseas, the group may collect needed supplies for them. When our fall group project was a church cookbook, we planned our January kickoff event as an unveiling tasting party for the cookbook. Because Scripture and a Christian witness were interspersed through the cookbook, we purchased extras to use with our outreach ministry team and community welcome ministry team.

Most group projects function best if an assigned person is in charge. An individual or team of women may take responsibility for the group project. One fall semester we collected new socks of all sizes for our benevolence ministry. The two women planning the project decorated a wicker laundry basket to collect the socks for the first two months of the semester. They hung the rolled pairs of socks with an ornament hook on a Christmas tree, and continued collecting socks until Christmas. The project was simple, and it met a need.

Ideas for Group Projects

Missionary encouragement	Send a care package to encourage a missionary or to help with a specific project.
Cookies for firemen, police, mayor	Deliver cookies and prayer notes.
Baptist Campus Ministries lunches	Prepare and serve lunch for nearby university students.
Coats for Christ/Jackets for Jesus	Collect and distribute blankets or warm clothing for benevolence project.
Christmas glove tree or sock tree	Collect socks for benevolence, roll as ornaments on a Christmas tree.
Church beautification project	Enjoy a brown bag lunch and flower-planting party.
Community Easter egg hunt	Collect candies; each woman hangs six flyers; delivers six egg invitations.
Cookbook	Create a cookbook with a Christian witness.
Community love letters	Everyone signs a prayer note to a community leader weekly.
Heart to Heart	Pair women for mentoring friendships.
Crisis project	If a community crisis occurs, rise to the task.

First day of school moms' brunch	Plan a prayer brunch for all moms in town after they drop kids at school.
Emergency waiting room basket	Add a prayer note to a huge snack basket for the waiting room; refill regularly.
Lambs for children's hospital	Collect lambs for a hospital chaplain to deliver to children. Add prayer notes.
Live nativity scene	Individuals sew a costume for an upcoming event.
Lottie Moon high tea	Plan a fancy Christmas tea as a foreign missions fund-raiser.
Love notes	Plaster staff's office walls with encouragement notes written on sticky pads.
Shield a Badge with Prayer	This is a planned commitment to pray for local police. (See www.namb.net.)
Shower for church kitchen, nursery, or pro-life clinic	Collect gifts for the entire semester.
Project: Jesus Loves the Little Children	Plan a huge August benevolent giveaway of school supplies, backpacks, clothing, and haircuts.
Snacks or meal for construction workers	Prepare snacks for nearby workers or students.
Truck and doll drive	Collect specific toys for a benevolence project.
The Great Giveaway	Plan a huge garage sale as a witness; everything is free!
Treat the Teachers	Collect goodies for a lovely snack basket and prayer notes for teachers at a nearby school.

Remember the old television commercial where they said, "Give it to Mikey. He will eat anything." If your women's ministry is truly effective, that's what will happen. When there's a need around the church, they'll say, "Just ask our women's ministry; they'll help with anything!"

Work hard to build a reputation for joyful service.

Small Church Tip

Here's an area where a small church can shine! Choose group projects carefully, fitting them to meet needs in your immediate community and church. Some projects may involve the Girls in Action or another girls' group in your church. A small church could plan a mission trip for women in the church.

Are You Ready?

I trudged through the Sabine National Forest's big thicket, cloaked in my bright yellow "victim chaplain" jacket. It was just after the space shuttle disaster, and I was part of a search line of forest rangers, FBI, NASA, and firefighters—all spaced ten feet apart. When we stopped, exhausted, for lunch, we found a special treat in our lunch bags—a huge homemade cookie, with a small, typed note:

"Jesus said, 'Come to me, all you who are weary and burdened, and I will give you rest.'

We're praying for you today. First Baptist Church of Hemphill."

Women in that small rural church had not expected such a tragedy in their town, but they immediately found a way to share God's love during a crisis situation.
   Be ready for unexpected opportunities.

CHAPTER 13

Special Events

Let your graciousness be known to everyone.
—**Philippians 4:5**

An occasional special event can add oomph with purpose to your women's ministry program. Over the years women's events at our church have included annual retreats, women's conferences, missions emphases, mission trips, and luncheons. A special event adds a boost of energy and excitement. It provides another easy entry point for newcomers and involves additional women in short-term leadership roles. It may meet needs that would otherwise not be met. Special events can greatly enhance a women's ministry program.

Select the type of event you want to implement, read everything you can find about the topic, and plan it well.

In our model women's ministry program, the key special event was a quarterly ladies' luncheon. For illustrative purposes, this chapter will detail planning for the luncheons. This same planning process may be used for most other special events.

Ladies' Luncheons for Outreach

It was greatly anticipated. Ladies bought tickets weeks in advance, scrambling for the best seats. They were enthusiastic about inviting new acquaintances and unsaved friends. Our quarterly ladies' luncheons were one of our best church outreach programs.

Quote from Survey

"I buy two tickets for the luncheon, then I pray about who God wants me to invite."

THE PURPOSE

Our ladies luncheons are not growth seminars for Christians, not missionary education events, and not typical "women's club" programs. They are gorgeous and social and entertaining, but they have a spiritual purpose. It's a lively, enthusiastic atmosphere with an unintimidating opportunity to share about Christ. Its primary purpose is outreach. What makes a ladies' luncheon outreach? I'm glad you asked.

- All the glitz and fun of a luncheon help to create a venue to share Christ with women who don't know Him. Almost every luncheon resulted in new Christians and new church members.

- Each table hostess personally invites women to Sunday's worship and Bible study.

- An inspirational speaker tells how God impacts her daily life and unapologetically shares His plan of salvation.

- The most desirable tables are reserved for members who bring guests, gently reminding ladies to bring lost friends.

- The door prize entry form obtains contact information for follow-up. Women are invited to mark an X on the form if they want to learn more about becoming a Christian or joining the church.

Sample

```
┌─────────────────────────────────────────────────────────────┐
│                                                               │
│               Door Prize Entry Form  ❑                        │
│                                                               │
│   Name _____        │
│                                                               │
│   If you're a guest, please complete:                         │
│   Address _____ Zip _____      │
│   E-mail _____ Phone _____      │
│                                                               │
│   ❑ I'm looking for a church home.                            │
│   ❑ I'm an active member at another church.                   │
│   ❑ I'm interested in receiving information about:            │
│       ❑ Church events          ❑ Women's weekday classes      │
│       ❑ Sunday Bible study     ❑ Women's events               │
│       ❑ Teen activities        ❑ How to become a Christian    │
│       ❑ Children's activities  ❑ How to join the church       │
│                                                               │
└─────────────────────────────────────────────────────────────┘
```

THE LUNCHEON PLANNING TEAM

The luncheon coordinator forms a planning team made of a few energetic members of varying ages. She synchronizes the team and oversees the luncheon program. Each team member coordinates specific elements, such as decorations, promotion, food, table hostesses, tickets, child care, and prayer. A theme is carried through each lunch's promotion, program, music, and decor, resulting in a one-of-a-kind blessing.

In the LIGHT model, the luncheon coordinator is the only officer that is limited to one year of service. Four luncheons is an enormous task! One of her team members will likely take that responsibility next year.

Tickets are sold ahead of time. The price is affordable and covers most expenses. Our luncheon tickets cost six dollars, and we sold out regularly. When a woman gives a friend a ticket she purchased, it has more value, and the friend is more likely to join her.

Child care is provided to encourage mothers to attend. A printed note on the ticket asks them to call the church office for free or inexpensive child-care reservations and advises them if they need to bring a sack lunch for each child.

LUNCHEONS ARE PREDICTABLE

Set a high standard so your luncheons are predictable in these ways:

- *Predictably top quality.* Lavish care on every detail to create a first-class event. Printed name tags, small take-home gifts, lovely decorations, beautifully presented food, live background music—every detail shouts "special!" Because they know it will be top-notch, women will bring work associates, new neighbors, grandmothers, and unsaved friends.

- *Predictably scheduled.* Because you have a printed schedule of women's events for the year, the date is on women's calendars. It's simple for a woman to invite a guest. If she meets a new friend in the dental waiting room, grocery store, or board meeting, she can just check her calendar and invite her to the next luncheon.

- *Predictably timed.* Our mantra is, "We don't get a second chance to run overtime." One overtime luncheon will negatively impact subsequent attendance for years! Print a beginning and ending time, such as 11:30 a.m. to 1:00 p.m., on the tickets and then keep your promise. The pace is relaxed, but the timing is impeccable.

- *Predictably unpredictable.* A ten-minute mini-feature is often the wow factor for the luncheon. It might be a fashion show, demonstration, or unique presentation; and it often ties to the speaker's topic. Brainstorm your theme to make one thing memorable such as a gorgeous entry, surprise guest, or amazing dessert.

- *Predictably chocolate.* OK, this part is bribery, but the dessert is almost always chocolate. If a lemon tart is served, however, it would be appropriate to place a small chocolate mint at each setting. Don't knock it. It works.

THE LUNCHEON PROGRAM

The format for luncheons is consistent. The content is not. Each luncheon has a theme, and the program is built around it.

Luncheons begin with a greeting from the pastor's wife, an opening prayer, and an uninterrupted time of fellowship and eating. Sometimes a cold salad plate is preset on the tables. At other luncheons, table hostesses serve a hot meal to the ladies at their table. At still other luncheons, the food was served buffet style as women arrived. Whether food is prepared in-house or catered, the presentation is beautiful, and it is served expeditiously.

Each luncheon program contains a mini-feature—a brief, lively, special attraction, which is often heavily advertised. The mini-feature is usually just for fun and lasts only ten minutes. It may be a spring fashion show, tips about family traditions, or a cooking demonstration. The mini-feature often relates to the speaker's subject. Several examples are found on pages 128–130.

A special Christian music selection is presented before the speaker, using live accompaniment and the best musicians you can find. The song is carefully timed to fit the schedule. The speaker is given thirty or forty minutes, and part of her testimony will explain the plan of salvation. She may be an invited guest speaker or a well-prepared church member.

The final item on the program, the door prize, is a strategic element. The speaker or hostess asks women to complete their door prize entry form and invites women who would like to know more about Jesus to mark an X on their form. Those who mark an X are contacted that same afternoon (see sample door prize entry form on page 125). To expedite this process, only one wonderful door prize should be given. The prize may fit the theme, or it may be a one-time special item such as a quilt made by the quilting team. Table hostesses gather entries quickly, deposit them in a basket, and a name is drawn.

Decorations are always stunning but rarely costly. Decorate with Scripture, with members' unique collections, centerpieces, or seasonal flowers. I loved the Christmas luncheon when they used treasured nativity scenes from members for the centerpieces. Recruit your church's most gifted decorator, and watch her work magic. As you purchase basic decorating items such as vases, mirror tiles, and fabrics, store them in an organized closet for the entire church to borrow. Add at least one nice decor item to the permanent collection annually.

Is a ladies luncheon worthwhile? If just one woman is introduced to Jesus Christ as her Savior, it was worth all your effort.

And, as a bonus, they get chocolate!

Luncheon Theme Ideas

Theme/ Scripture	Decor Ideas	Mini-feature Ideas	Door Prize Idea	Extra Ideas Take-homes, Etc.
"Shine!" "Let your light shine before men" (Matt. 5:16).	Gather beautiful lights, i.e. decorative lanterns, lamps. Use oodles of lit candles.	Shoe shine lesson; drama during song; "Go Light Your World"	Tiffany lamp; fancy candle	Small reflectors; lightbulbs; tiny sunshine sticker to place on their lipstick to remind them to shine for Christ.
"Luncheon in Pink" "A beautiful woman who rejects good sense is like a gold ring in a pig's snout" (Prov. 11:22).	Pig decor/gold ring in snout could be loop earring. Lots of pink.	Pink fashion show or gold jewelry fashion show	Glass or porcelain pig	Order tiny plastic pigs; add gold rings in snouts; tie Scripture to it. Have a live pig in a pen at the entry.
"No Miniblinds in a Fishbowl" live out loud for Christ "Shine like stars" (Phil. 2:15).	Aquarium theme decor, live fish in floral arrangement container	Drapery demo; Demo of creating aquarium; glass house skit	Porcelain fish; Aquarium with fish	Giant blunt fishhooks with pin attachment; wear to remind us the world is observing; fish-shaped bookmark with Scripture
"Little Things Matter" "If you have faith the size of a mustard seed . . ." (Matt. 17:20).	Thimble collection; tiny decor; tiny flowers	"10 Little Tips"—cute ideas to make a difference; kids fashion show	Small valuable gift	Hershey kiss at place settings, gift in tiny box, mustard seed on Scripture bookmark.
"Let It Snow" "Casting all your care upon Him, because He cares about you" (1 Pet. 5:7). Speak on grief or stress.	Snow, lots of white, sparkle, hanging snowflakes. Rent snow machine.	Stress relief tips and demonstration	Snowball maker (looks like ice cream scoop), snowman kit, massage coupon	Stress relief booklet with Scriptures

More Luncheon Theme Ideas

Theme/ Scripture	Decor Ideas	Mini-feature Ideas	Door Prize Idea	Extra Ideas Take-homes, Etc.
"God Cares!" "Indeed, the hairs of your head are all counted" (Luke 12:7).	Porcelain bird collection and/or birdhouses (Luke 12:6)	Live haircuts on stage during dining. Show before and after photo (Luke 12:7).	Porcelain bird, bird feeder, bird house	Discount coupons for hair stylists featured.
"Vintage Lace" or "A Marriage Made in Heaven" Marriage or bride of Christ (Prov. 25:24; Eccl. 9:9).	Wedding theme decor, netting, white, arch entry or stage	Vintage wedding gown fashion show (older members' gowns modeled).	Anything white or lace	Display church members' wedding photographs at entry with one vintage gown on mannequin. Serve wedding cake for dessert.
"Joy in the Journey!" "Those who look to Him are radiant with joy" (Ps. 34:5).	Suitcases; flowers in makeup kits, smiley faces, "joy" decor from Christmas sales	Flight attendant demonstrates how to pack a suitcase, comedienne	Travel bag; "joy" wall hanging	Discretely drop a few boiled eggs in bags or pockets as ladies arrive. (Hilarious response!) Stack suitcases at entrance. Tickets resemble airline tickets.
"Better Than Chocolate" Knowing Christ is the greatest (Phil. 3:8).	Chocolate flowers, chocolate dessert as centerpiece	How-to demo for fancy chocolate dessert	Anything chocolate	Chocolate fondue or fountain for dessert
"Blue Is Beautiful" "Come to Me, . . . you who are weary" (Matt. 11:28).	Everything blue	Blue fashion show	Something blue, feather pillow (sleep)	Blues music
Royalty/Princess theme— child of the King "You are no longer a slave, but . . . an heir through God" (Gal. 4:7).	Lots of glitz and jewels	Fashion demo—dress like a million on a pauper's budget	Costume jewelry	Order tiny glass slipper from wedding Web sites, attach Scripture.

Got the idea? You'll come up with better themes than these. Begin with a Scripture and brainstorm.

Yearlong Luncheon Theme Ideas

For a change we planned a yearlong theme, and it worked great. Each stand-alone lunch fit the all-year theme.

All-Year Theme	Scripture	Luncheon Topics	Extras
"Dress for Success" (Armor of God)	Ephesians 6	Each lunch focused on one piece of armor, i.e. shoes, belt, vest	A mannequin on stage modeled the belt, etc.
"Seasons"	Ecclesiastes 3:1	Each theme was tied to the season—fall, winter, summer, spring	Living room scene on stage changed seasons
"Fruit of the Spirit"	Galatians 5:22	Each luncheon focused on one or more of the fruits of the Spirit	Fruit desserts

Luncheon Planning Worksheet

Theme/ Scripture	Decor Ideas	Mini-feature Ideas	Door Prize Ideas	Extras

The story continues . . .

Our luncheons ministered to hundreds of women over the years, and many women made eternity-impacting decisions for Christ. It's been many years since I attended that first, smaller church where we began women's ministry and outreach luncheons. The church continues to grow, and it's no small church anymore.

The church secretary called me last Christmas and said, "Guess what! We had four hundred women at our Christmas luncheon!"

Once upon a Holiday

I recently attended an excellent example of a fun, purposeful special event. Calvary Baptist (a medium-sized church in Greenwood, Indiana), hosted their second annual "Once upon a Holiday" event, a Friday evening/Saturday morning Christmas-themed conference in mid-November.

A huge outdoor banner invited the community, and members of the church invited all their friends. The $10 cost included evening snacks and Saturday luncheon. The event was scheduled in mid-November before the holiday hustle, and ladies flocked to it.

Friday's program included a well-known inspirational speaker, a fabulous singer, and an amazing dramatic monologue, all followed by a Seasonal Sweets fellowship. Women could select three Saturday-morning workshops before the holiday luncheon. Workshops were all about Christmas fun, and every class culminated with Christ! Look at this workshop list:

Magic menus	Cookie gift boxes
Gingerbread houses	Gifts in a jar
Simply Christmas	Family traditions (teens)
Gift wrapping	Christmas trees
Family traditions (children)	Holiday menus
Setting the scene	Handling grief and depression
Tastes of fall	Christmas beading
Celebrating Advent as a family	Wreath making
Holiday decorating	Decorating with nativities

The event culminated in a beautiful Christmas luncheon with an entertaining speaker who shared the gospel. It took a major effort, but God honored this purposeful special event.

Small Church Tip

Consider planning a special event to include other churches in your immediate area. A small church in Indiana plans a fabulous women's conference for all the churches in their town. Another small church invites all the churches in their region to an annual mother-daughter luncheon. Another small church invites other churches to attend an excellent women's retreat with scheduled time for individual church fellowship. Take a group from your church to a statewide or regional event for women. There are wonderful opportunities for special events. Watch for them!

CHAPTER 14

Publicize

Invite everyone you find to the banquet.
                                        —Matthew 22:9

An intentional plan for publicity is essential. If they don't know, they won't go. It often takes eight separate publicity points for an announcement to be noticed. An excellent publicity plan considers a separate strategy for two distinct groups:

- Women inside the church—current women's ministry participants, church members who aren't involved in women's ministry, and Sunday visitors to your church
- Women outside the church—friends of church members and women in your community who don't attend church

The promotion coordinator will make a dated yearlong publicity plan. By calendaring due dates for promotions such as church newsletter, signage, and local newspaper deadlines, publicity is more likely to be timely. The largest promotion event is for the fall kickoff. However, ongoing promotional strategies will be implemented for luncheons, events, projects, and new mid-semester classes. For example, four weeks before a luncheon, posters are hung and a small article appears in the church newsletter. Three weeks before, ticket sales begin, an exterior banner is erected, and local newspaper publicity begins. Two weeks before, an invitation is distributed to women at church.

The promotion coordinator may delegate responsibilities to capable assistants, making use of their skills and contacts. The quality of printed and visual materials will impact expectations. Slipshod posters will give a clue that the program may not be worthwhile. Women with computer graphics talents and artistic abilities can make any event look good!

One secret to quality, effective promotion happens well before the advertising campaign begins. Because you have carefully created an annual schedule to provide multiple entry points, the chance of including newcomers is multiplied! Your publicity plan should include additional exposure before each of those entry points.

When a woman meets a new friend, there is always a new opportunity to invite her to the women's program. Just think about it. In our LIGHT model, there are ten obvious entry points for newcomers, and each provides an opportunity for publicity:

- The next kickoff event—fall or spring
- The first official day of LIGHT—fall or spring
- The next luncheon—fall, Christmas, spring, May
- New midsemester classes—fall or spring

The story continues . . .

We'd worked hard to develop our purpose statement and overall program. As we began a publicity plan, someone suggested that our women's ministry needed a name. And so our future women's ministry leaders met together for a name brainstorming session.

To prepare for the meeting, all officers spent time in prayer. Their assignment was to bring a minimum of three written ideas for a women's ministry name. Even if they weren't great, they had to bring three. We wanted our name to reflect our purpose, so each was given a written copy of our purpose statement.

A brainstorming meeting is just that, a storm of brains! Every idea was written on a whiteboard, and then we discussed them, tweaking some slightly, giggling about a few, and eliminating others. Some were boring. Others were too long. Some were tongue twisters. One member loved acronym names, and we came up with some doozies. As we talked, one word kept resurfacing—*light*. We'd chosen Matthew 5:16 for our theme Scripture, "Let your light shine."

When our brainstorming session ended, we had eliminated every suggestion. But more important, we had agreed that we would call our group LIGHT, and we would gather for another brainstorming session to come up with acronym words to fit. Again each officer was to bring three suggestions, and even kids and husbands helped.

At our second brainstorming session, we plastered the walls with five huge blank flipchart pages, one for each letter of *light*. As each person shared her acronym words, we wrote the *L* words on the *L* page, the *I* words on the *I* page, and so on. Ultimately, we agreed on these words:

Ladies
Intentionally
Going,
Helping,
Touching

For ease of promotion, we wrote it with capital letters—LIGHT. It was a great women's ministry name for several reasons:

- It's short. It's simple to use in promotion and verbal invitations.
- It's descriptive of our purpose—lighting our world for Christ.
- It sounds inviting. "Come to LIGHT!"
- It lends itself to visuals: rays of light, lightbulb, sunshine.
- It's cheerful and easy to remember.

And the final test: the pastor loved it. Our women's ministry name was found.

Name It and Brand It

Naming your women's ministry is a one-time project, but it will enhance publicity thereafter. If you're beginning a new women's ministry program, put significant effort into naming and branding it.

How would your new infant feel if you decided not to give her a name? If you decide just to call her "our child" or "our daughter." Perhaps you could do that legally, but it's much more personal and practical to choose a lovely, meaningful name for your daughter.

Ditto for your women's ministry program. Give it a meaningful, inviting name. The ideal name for your women's ministry will be short, inviting, and descriptive of your purpose. This is important. Do it well.

Take a look at these potential names for a women's ministry:

- "Women of Main Street Baptist's Evangelistic and Missionary Bible Enrichment Group"—This one is descriptive but difficult. The acronym, WMSBEMBEG, doesn't work either.

- "WAG" (acronym for Women in Action for God)—It's simple, short, and descriptive; but the acronym WAG has little to do with the group purpose and is rather uninviting.

- "You Go Girl"—This one might actually work. It indicates that the group is for females and suggests action.

- "Holy Hands of Mirth"—Though descriptive and short, this name may not entice or easily communicate with a woman of this century.

When you've decided on a title, say it out loud to evaluate its appeal. For example, which phrase would you prefer to say to a newcomer?

"I'd love to invite you to the Women of Main Street Baptist's Evangelistic and Missionary Bible Enrichment Group," or, "I'd love to invite you to LIGHT."

Some no-no's:

- Don't name the women's ministry after a person. The single purpose of your women's ministry is to serve and honor God, not a person.

- No negatives. "Women against . . ." or "Better than last year's . . ." type names do nothing to reflect God's love.

- No long and burdensome names. Brief is better. If the name is long, be sure it has a good nickname or acronym.

And finally, brand it. Ask an artistic member to design a logo for your women's ministry or select appropriate clip art and use it on every announcement, program, and promotion. Select a consistent font for the title. Make a trip to the office supply store and choose a unique paper color, such as hot pink. Write "women's ministry copies only" on the reams of paper in the church office, and use that color for every printed announcement page, women's ministry newsletter, name tag, and promotion piece (see a sample on page 177).

Publicity Inside the Church

Everybody's talking about LIGHT! In the young adult Sunday school class. In the hallways at church. At the PTA meeting and the community center. It's sort of like good gossip, if there is such a thing.

A promotion coordinator's goal is to create a buzz. How do you get that kind of talking started? How can you promote your women's ministry inside the church?

WOMEN'S MINISTRY BROCHURE

The single most important document for promotion is the women's ministry brochure. The promotion coordinator gathers details for classes, ministry teams, and calendar dates and compiles a brochure. As with every printed document, the church and pastor's name and church Web site are prominent.

Copies of the brochures are available in visible locations in the church building and are included in new-member packets and visitor information.

If your group prints a women's ministry newsletter or e-newsletter (see a sample on page 146), that document could also be used for the same purposes.

CHURCH PUBLICATIONS

Use the church's bulletins, newsletter, announcement sheets, audiovisual announcements, and Web site to make timely announcements. Reword each week's notice using short, concise wording. A new surge of publicity can accompany each entry point as luncheons, projects or new classes, and ministries begin. A brief monthly story highlighting different ministry teams may fit your church's newsletter.

VISUALS

Promotional flyers and posters must reflect the quality of your women's ministry program. A talented woman can create signs and displays using computer graphics or artistic ability. Many churches advertise in the ladies' restrooms and on elevators. Recruit artistic women to design bulletin boards and signs.

You could use an annual promotional theme and design publicity around it. For example, a lightbulb was used for one year's "LIGHT Your World" theme. Lightbulbs were used for all kinds of displays, such as flower arrangements, a visual with several bulbs hanging from a ceiling, and attached to posters. Every time women saw a lightbulb, they knew it was promoting women's ministry.

PULPIT PROMOTION

If your women's ministry is positively impacting your church, the pastor and staff will notice. If announcements are made during worship, provide written, up-to-date details of upcoming events. If you use a promotional skit, it should be first-class and less than a minute.

PERSONAL INVITATION

A dozen bulletin announcements and cute posters aren't as effective as one individual woman inviting another. Many women will never attend unless they are invited personally. Here's an idea for an almost-personal invitation. Ask a scrapbooker to design and prepare special invitations for an annual event such as the Christmas luncheon. Invite friendly women of all ages to distribute invitations to women leaving worship, along with a smile and encouragement to attend.

SUNDAY SCHOOL AMBASSADORS

Ask a woman from each Sunday school department or small group at your church to serve as a representative to invite women in her group to attend. Call or send an e-mail to remind her of upcoming events.

Small Church Tip

Don't be dismayed when you look at the seven-week bulletin handout on pages 142–143. Create your own handout. If you have three ministry teams with two women on each team, your chart may read like this: 10 hospital visits, 14 welcome packets delivered, 3 homebound contacts, 1 care package mailed to our Mexico missionary, Bible study of 1 John completed, etc. Each touch made in Jesus' name has an impact. When people read about the results of your ministry teams, they'll want to be a part, and your women's ministry will grow. Your church may be small, but your God isn't.

NEWCOMERS AT CHURCH

Encourage women to seek out and invite newcomers at church to attend the women's ministry. They can offer to meet them at the entrance. Assign someone to call every first-time guest at your church within three days of her visit to invite her to the women's ministry.

DISPLAY RACKS

Print a women's ministry newsletter or calendar and put copies in the church foyer, display racks, and newcomer and guest packets.

PHONE TREE

A phone tree may be used sparingly to remind women of important events. Personal calls are even better.

WORTHWHILE PUBLICITY

An occasional bulletin insert may be prepared to demonstrate the effectiveness of your women's ministry. Pages 142–143 show a bulletin insert, detailing specific numbers of ministry contacts and inviting women to attend.

The story continues . . .

Divide and conquer. Our leadership team had made a commitment to personally invite every female member of our church to attend women's ministry. We printed a church membership list, marked off the women who already attended the women's ministry, and our officers initialed the names they would contact. At the next officers' meetings each person made a report.

Erma was on my list. I didn't know her at all, but she had been a longtime church member. When I telephoned, she enthusiastically accepted my invitation to LIGHT. She chatted about her love for doll collecting and making porcelain doll faces, and I felt like I already had a new friend.

Erma knew just how to make newcomers welcome, and soon she was joyfully serving as a greeter for LIGHT. After she became involved, Erma led a class to teach doll making, and our luncheon team used her doll collection for table decorations. One phone call made a difference.

Sample Midsemester Bulletin Insert

What happened in First Baptist's Ladies' LIGHT during the first seven weeks?

- Enrolled 158 women in ministry teams and classes.
- Enrolled 54 preschoolers in GLO (God's Little Ones) class.
- Made 26 homebound, 21 hospital, and 50 nursing home visits.
- Lost 42½ pounds in First Place class.
- Delivered 112 meals and sermon tapes to senior adults.
- Welcomed 26 young moms to preschool moms Bible study.
- Prayed for 840 of our missionaries on their birthday.
- Prepared 200 dolls and lots of toys for Christmas benevolence.
- Wrote 151 notes of Christian encouragement in Quill Ministry.
- Created topiaries, birdhouses, and paintings in craft classes.
- Graded/counseled 230 prisoners' Bible studies.
- Learned hundreds of truths from 28 chapters of God's Word.
- Communicated online with 5 missionaries and 12 collegeans.
- Assigned 150 heart-to-heart prayer partners.
- Worked 70 woman-hours at our Friendship House (benevolence).
- Reproduced and mailed 246 worship tapes.
- Mentored with 7 students, encouraged 7 new moms.
- 12 women are learning signed English, 12 learning Spanish.
- Delivered 28 welcome-to-worship packets to new city residents.
- Averaged 120 women in LIGHT weekly attendance.

LIGHT

Ladies Intentionally Going, Helping, and Touching

Want to get involved in this worthwhile women's ministry?
You're needed!

Complete the other side of this page and turn it in at the church welcome desk. See you Thursday, 9:30 a.m. to Noon, in Room 190.

LIGHT the Next Seven Weeks

Register today. Classes and ministry teams begin this Thursday at 9:30 a.m.

EnLIGHTening CLASSES   9:30 a.m Thursdays beginning
                                                                October 15

❏ Signing as a Second Language
❏ *How Much Is Enough?* Finance Bible study
❏ Women on Mission
❏ Christmas wreath-making class
❏ Christian book reviews
❏ Rubber-stamping for holidays
❏ *The Book of Daniel* (continued)
❏ *First Place* Bible study (continued)

MINISTRY TEAMS 10:30 a.m. Thursdays beginning October 15
❏ Christmas House Team—Prepare toys for needy children.
❏ Welcome Team—Deliver welcome packets to new residents.
❏ School Mentoring Team—Work one-on-one with at-risk students.
❏ Nursing Home Team—Share smiles and God's love with patients.
❏ Nursing Home Melody Team—Share Christian music.
❏ Prison Bible Correspondence—Make a difference for inmates.
❏ Homebound Team—Make personal visits to shut-ins.
❏ Friendship House Team—Help with benevolence food and
    clothing.
❏ LIGHT Online Team—Encourage missionaries and college
    students.
❏ Love Crafts Team—Make gifts for ministry team distribution.
❏ Hospital Ministry Team—Make visits to the sick.
❏ Meals on Wheels Team—Deliver food and Scriptures to shut-ins.
❏ Quill Ministry—Write personal notes of encouragement.
❏ Tape Ministry—Duplicate and mail worship tapes.

Put this registration form in the offering plate today.

Name _____ **Phone** _____

Publicity Outside the Church

A women's ministry can be well planned, purposeful, and implemented perfectly; but if new people are not included, it's just a club! Make an intentional bring-'em-in plan to invite outsiders to come inside.

FRIENDSHIP INVITATIONS

The most effective way to reach women who do not attend church is by personal invitation. Design ways to help members invite friends easily.

- *Wear T-shirts*. Print LIGHT T-shirts for women to order for an effortless way to advertise.

- *Business cards work*. They're inexpensive and effective. Print an attractive women's ministry business card with your church and pastor's name, church address, Web site, and a women's ministry schedule. Give cards to every women's ministry participant, and encourage her to invite friends and new acquaintances (see a sample on page 90).

- *Forward this*. Design a computer-generated invitation to the women's ministry program or special event. E-mail it to all participants with instructions to forward it to friends who may want to attend.

- *Take two*. When distributing or mailing semester schedules for women's ministry, give each member two copies. Encourage her to share the schedule with a friend.

MASS INVITATIONS

You may consider mass mailings to invite your community to a quality event or to inform them about your women's program. One semester we mailed or delivered invitations to a women's event to every home within four blocks of our church building.

Outdoor advertising may be worthwhile. Use your church's changeable sign or create an outdoor banner invitation.

LOCAL NEWSPAPERS

Many local newspapers will print community interest stories or photographs. Watch for interesting stories and photos, and submit a brief article and digital photo. For example, our local paper used a group shot of ladies in wedding dresses at a bride-themed luncheon. An overhead shot of a fair-themed kickoff made a great newspaper photo. Our local paper often printed a photo of our guest speaker for an event, along with an invitation, such as, "All women of Redstone are invited to attend the May 29 luncheon. Make reservations at . . ."

Community listings provide an excellent means to invite newcomers to events or classes. Select one or two aspects of your program that would interest outsiders, such as a weight-loss Bible study or quilting class. Include registration details and contact information.

Always approve the article through your church office before submitting it. Include the name of a contact person for additional information, along with the church's name, address, phone, Web site, and pastor's name. Don't become discouraged if articles are not printed. Continue to submit them. They may need a filler *next* week!

If your women's group is the best kept secret in town, change that concept! A vibrant women's program can, and should, impact your church's growth.

Small Church Tip

Publicize well. Your women's ministry should impact church growth even more than a large church! Create opportunities for members to involve friends and acquaintances in ministries and classes. When a guest arrives at women's ministry, stop visiting with your old buddies and show God's love to the newcomer. Make a rule that every first-time attender will get at least one invitation out for lunch that week. Plan at least one outreach event to include new people each semester.

Sample Newsletter

Humorist Ethel Sexton headlines Oct. 2 luncheon

Expect a blessing and a lot of laughs!

Aittle saucy. . . a little sassy. . . really, really cute and funny. . . captivating.

If you expect anything less than all of this when you attend the Oct. 2 L.I.G.H.T. luncheon, you will get a big disappointment! Ethel Sexton, humorist, entertainer and eclectic entrepreneur, will not only tickle your funny bone, she will also get to your heart with her inspiration and philosophies about living life to the fullest.

Some of you may know this "Texas original" as "the garage sale lady". . . or maybe the "Make Your Own Sunshine lady." Whatever your impression at the moment, just know that you will walk away with a little of that sunshine in your heart that day. . . and many will probably plan a weekend garage sale attack before the day is over.

And don't forget about the other "specials" of the day: the music, the food, the fellowship with new friends.

Buy your ticket now for only $5. We'd hate to miss you because of a "sell-out" crowd that left no tickets for those who waited until the last minute!

L.I.G.H.T.

Ladies Involved in Going, Helping, Touching

Week of Prayer
for state missions

September 14-21

• Use your prayer guide in your Sunday's bulletin to guide your family

• Give to our special offering (FBC's goal: $30,000)

Congrats!
L.I.G.H.T.bulb Award recipients

Mae Kimmel
Francis Huff
Sandra Zercher
Eudean Page

Be a 'friend' that helps in times of need

♥ First Baptist Garland loves and supports its Friendship House. We appreciate the work Susan Boyd, director, and her many volunteers do to help those in need in the our community.

For those of you waiting for word on how you can help next, it's time to line up at the grocery store. "August was a huge month for food needs," Susan said. Friendship House fed over 229 families—that's over 900 people—so the food closet needs replenishing. Friendship House relies on the FBC family to keep them stocked with staple goods.

Also, keep the approaching holiday season in mind. Because so many families have so little, Christmas gifts are hard to come by. Go ahead and start buying toys and gift items for children and teens.

For "a terrific idea," be sure to read the column on the back. Susan has an idea of how you can get your children involved in this wonderful ministry.

Oct. 2
L.I.G.H.T. Luncheon

Childcare

Call the church office for reservations

Send a sack lunch; no lunches will be provided for the children

BREAD BREAD BREAD

Make it. Bake it. Deliver it straight to the Welcome Ministry (or the registration table). Their need is great!

CHAPTER 15

Evaluations

If we were properly evaluating ourselves, we would not be judged.
—1 Corinthians 11:31

We're not finished until we've evaluated and updated. In this chapter we'll discuss the importance of year-end evaluations and reporting to the church.

The story continues . . .

The stage for our Christmas luncheon was decorated one year with twelve enormous gift-wrapped boxes stacked in a pyramid. In large letters on the front of each box was written the name of a different ministry team and the number of ministry contacts made that semester. "Homebound Ministry: 12 Personal Visits." The banner above the display read, "Our gift to Jesus."

Record-keeping can help draw a visual picture of ministry that's worth a thousand words.

Keeping Records

The hospitality coordinator gathers weekly statistics such as attendance, names of guests, individual class and ministry team attendance, and ministry team visits and submits a brief monthly and annual report to the church office. An annual report includes a roster of members and guests and brief ministry summaries. She devises a simple method of collecting the information either on a form, a chart at the church, or by e-mail. Why keep records? Four reasons:

- *Celebrate.* By keeping records, you have cause to celebrate often. The missions group has its highest attendance in history. Your hospital team visited one hundred patients. The fiftieth woman joins women's ministry, and you're ready with a bouquet and gift to celebrate when she arrives.

- *Encouragement.* For example, one small class or ministry, viewed alone, may seem insignificant. However, when everyone sees the big picture of women's ministry, it takes on a larger importance.

- *Effectiveness.* Record-keeping can enhance the outreach effectiveness of the church. By sharing contact information with the church office, guests will receive additional contacts. By graphing attendance, officers will be aware if attendance declines or stagnates.

- *Focus.* By spotlighting ministry numbers, a reminder is given about the Acts 1:8 purpose of your women's ministry. One semester we printed a half-semester sheet (see page 142) to show the impact of our women's ministry. On the reverse side was an invitation for ladies to attend along with a list of classes and ministry teams. We distributed it on Sunday and had a record number of new visitors the next week!

Annual Evaluation Form

Women love to give their opinion. Use the sample form on pages 150–151 to design a year-end evaluation form. The evaluations should be completed anonymously. Leave plenty of room for written comments. Distribute the forms each week during the last month of your ministry year. Mail an evaluation form to every woman who attended even once during the year. Invite women to deposit their form in a collection basket, return it by mail, or complete it online.

By aggressively gathering year-end evaluations, the leadership team communicates that they are listening to women who attend. But mere listening isn't enough. After tabulating evaluations, they must go to work to *make changes* to enhance the ministry even further. Nothing is set in stone except the purpose statement.

The story continues . . .

After looking through reams of evaluation forms from years of women's ministry, I can truthfully say that our leadership team implemented the vast majority of suggestions offered. Throughout this book you've read comments from those evaluation forms. Our leadership team reveled in those compliments, but critical comments and constructive criticism helped us improve our women's ministry program every year.

For example, when our missions group felt confined with our one-hour class schedule, our leadership team polled the fellowship class leaders and determined to begin women's ministry at 9:00 a.m. instead of 9:30 at the beginning of the next year. A few years later those same groups determined that the one-hour format was better. Again we came to a consensus, and women's ministry began that next year at 9:30 a.m. Small adjustments can make an enormous difference.

By listening carefully and responding prayerfully to suggestions, your women's ministry program can stay current and fresh. Don't fret about receiving negative feedback. Remember, you aren't fishing for compliments. The purpose of evaluation forms is to request suggestions for improvements.

Rick Warren says it like this on pastors.com, "Praise and criticism are like bubble gum. You chew on them, but you don't swallow them." Enjoy the compliments, chew on the constructive criticism, and use both as stepping stones to improve next year's plan.

A separate year-end volunteer survey (see the sample on page 153) may be taken to discover potential leadership for the coming year. It lists every possible area where assistance may be needed.

Small Church Tip

Evaluate or stagnate. This is where you must think like a big church. Try any reasonable suggestion given on evaluation forms. If you've been doing things the same way for years and you're not reaching new people, perhaps it's time to try something totally new. Honor God in every new venture, and reach newcomers in His name. Evaluate and update!

LIGHT Year Evaluation

Please take a few minutes to give your honest, anonymous evaluation and input. Please return this form by mail or put in the suggestion box. Watch for more women's ministry improvements next fall!

My favorite thing about LIGHT is: _____

My least favorite thing about LIGHT is: _____

Yes/No   Do you have a child in GLO? Comment: _____

Yes/No   Did you attend LIGHT regularly? Comment: _____

Yes/No   Did you participate in a ministry team? Comment: ____

Yes/No   Did you attend a fellowship class? Comment: _____

Yes/No   Did you attend a LIGHT luncheon? Comment: _____

Yes/No   Did you bring a friend to a luncheon? Comment: _____

Yes/No   Did you make new friends at LIGHT? Comment: _____

Circle the comments below that reflect your opinion of LIGHT.

Worth my time   Helps me grow spiritually
Well-planned classes   Helps me meet friends
Effective ministry teams   I love the luncheons
Highlight of my week   Enhances my missions awareness
Boring   Helps me be a more effective Christian

Write a brief evaluation comment or improvement suggestion about:

Overall schedule _____

Fellowship classes (choices, effectiveness) _____

Coffee break food and fellowship _____

Ministry teams _____

Luncheons _____

My age group is (circle one): 20s 30s 40s 50s 60s 70s 80s+

One way LIGHT might reach more women my age is:_____
_____

I am: __ a member of First Baptist Church
         __ a regular attender but not a member
         __ a member of a different church, an attender at LIGHT
         __ not a member of any church

Share ideas for group projects, ministries, studies, comments, etc. on the back of this form. Thanks!

Ministry Team Evaluation

Name (optional) _____

Your opinions and ideas are extremely important. Please share them!

My current ministry team is (circle one):

Clothes closet	Cradle roll	Hospital
Food pantry	LIGHT brigade	Love crafts
Prayer walk	Quill	Homebound
Welcome	Nursing home	Tape

I've enjoyed being on this ministry team because _____

_____

Do you feel we should continue this ministry next fall?   Yes No

Ideas to improve this ministry team: _____

_____

Suggestion for a new ministry team (must fit Matt. 25:35–36):

_____

Would you like to lead a class or ministry team? ____ Which? ____

Suggestion for new craft or Bible class: _____

Suggestion for ministry team or class leader: _____

My favorite thing about LIGHT is: _____

Let your light shine!

Individual areas may occasionally survey. In our model women's program, for example, ministry team members were surveyed to help determine which teams to reschedule for the next semester.

Sample Year-end Volunteer Form

Next LIGHT Year

Please check any areas where you would consider serving next fall.

Name: _____

Weekly Jobs
❑ Serve as an officer _____
❑ Coordinate snacks for break time
❑ Assist with weekly snack setup or cleanup
❑ Weekly greeter (arrive at 9:15 a.m.)
❑ Lead a ministry team _____
❑ Lead an existing ministry team (openings for hospital and outreach teams)
❑ Call first-time guests at our church each week to invite them to LIGHT
❑ Call first-timers to LIGHT to thank them for attending
❑ Lead a crafts class _____
❑ Help with a buddy system for newcomers to LIGHT
❑ Participant
❑ Other _____

Short-Term Jobs
❑ Cookbook team
❑ Photography
❑ LIGHT mail-out
❑ Newsletter
❑ Prepare coffee
❑ Make posters
❑ Greeter
❑ Luncheon setup
❑ Photographer

❑ Luncheon hostess
❑ LIGHT directory
❑ Computer or graphic arts
❑ Posters/bulletin boards
❑ Assist a ministry leader
❑ Snacks for one week
❑ Community publicity
❑ Luncheon cleanup
❑ Sell lunch tickets

❑ Help plan "Tasting Tea" to unveil cookbook
❑ Coordinate project/snacks for construction workers
❑ Assist with doing luncheon decorations (four Wednesday evenings)
❑ I know someone who might enjoy teaching GLO next fall. Call me.
❑ An area of expertise where I can volunteer _____

CHAPTER 16

Postlude

He who started a good work in you will carry it to completion.
—**Philippians 1:6**

Whew! You've successsfully begun a vibrant women's ministry in your church. Women are learning from God's Word. They're supporting missions. They're involved in hands-on community ministry and outreach projects. Christian friendships are flourishing and your church is growing. The first year has been a true, amazing blessing.

Did you notice that this book has detailed ten essential planning steps? Those same planning and implementation steps will be repeated every year as a cyclical process. It looks like this:

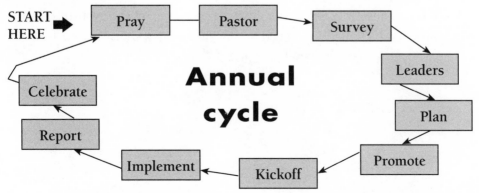

Want a sixty-second summary?

Pray hard. God is listening.

Ask the pastor. God called him to lead your church.

Take a survey and listen well.

Visionary leaders make a great women's ministry.

Plan well. It's time well spent.

Publicize or go home.

Kickoff in a big way to begin well.

Elevate ministry. Be doers of the Word.

Evaluate and report. Tweak it for improvement.

Celebrate! Thank God for His blessings.

Begin again!

The story continues . . .

Our women's ministry was still going strong after many productive years. It positively impacted the lives of many women. It helped grow our church. It even changed our church's reputation in the community.

When God moved my husband and me to serve in a different city, I was sad to leave our great women's program. At our new, larger church, fewer than a dozen ladies regularly attended the various weekday women's groups. Once again, the leaders of those miniscule pieces of women's ministries expressed a desire to unite and improve. Once again, we began with prayer.

As planning progressed, I started to fret. I realized that this large church's women's ministry might actually be smaller than at our former church. We were all amazed when more than three hundred women were involved in LIGHT and NightLIGHT during the first semester. And it's still going strong a decade later.

Minichurch or megachurch—women's ministry works!

Are you convinced? A women's ministry can be one of the best things happening in your church! If God has called you to this ministry, invest your best efforts. Remember, there are great eternal benefits.

Pointing to Jesus

My daughter, Autumn, was the Garland High School mascot. She wore a big furry costume and a gigantic owl head, and entertained the crowds as Ollie the Owl. The high school had a cute tradition involving the mascot.

At the end of every ball game, whether they won or lost, the owl would stand in the middle of the field with wings spread. The entire stadium of spectators would rise, extend their arms, and point at the owl while the band played the school song.

Just imagine. A couple of thousand people, arms extended, pointing at an *owl* for a full four or five minutes! They were demonstrating their school spirit, but it made me think . . .

What would happen if every Christian woman in our church, all at the same time, decided to point to *Jesus?* Right in front of the whole world, we would stand up and point toward our Savior. No proud fingers pointing at ourselves, at our pastor or buildings, or at our families or belongings. Just pointing at Jesus.

That's what women's ministry is all about.

Now, if you've read to this point, it's time to put down this book and go to work. Blessings on you, and keep on shining!

Checklist for Women's Ministry Coordinator

		Page
❑	Realistically assess current women's programs at your church.	10
❑	Read everything you can find about women's ministry.	175
❑	Meet with your pastor.	15
❑	Secure pastoral approval and enthusiasm.	19
❑	Design a purpose statement.	21
❑	Design a survey.	22
❑	Take an all-church survey.	23
❑	Evaluate survey results.	25
❑	Determine meeting day of the week, time, frequency.	42
❑	Make calls to invite potential leaders to informational tea.	25
❑	Design leadership interest survey.	26
❑	Hold an informational tea.	25
❑	Evaluate potential leaders; make a list of possible leadership team.	29
❑	Meet with the pastor before recruiting leaders.	33

❑ Recruit leadership team; begin with ministry coordinator.   34

❑ Plan an informal gathering for the new leadership team.   35

❑ Give women's ministry a name.   136

❑ Determine proposed weekly schedule.   42

❑ Offer a mini-marathon meeting for annual planning.   44

❑ Approve dates through the church office.   49

❑ Compile an overall list of the leadership team and other leaders.   39

❑ Oversee the kickoff event planning (delegate responsibilities).   53

❑ Make sure child-care details are in place.   115

❑ Select this semester's group project; assign a leader for it.   119

❑ Assure details for brochure are submitted to publicity team.   135

❑ Check in with the leadership team members to assist and encourage.   30

❑ Plan leadership team meetings.   36

❑ Watch for training opportunities for leaders.   30

❑ Regularly report to pastor or staff liaison.   30

❑ Plan spring marathon planning meeting.   46

❑ Assure and assist the leadership team as they recruit assistants.   30

❑ Make a plan for yearlong prayer partners or mentors.   71

❑ Plan coffee break weekly dismissal.   72

❑ Prepare year-end evaluations.   150

APPENDIX 2

Checklist for Luncheon Coordinator

❏ Recruit an enthusiastic planning team.   125

❏ Meet with team to plan year themes, speakers, menu,
mini-specials, music.   128

❏ Submit luncheon theme and speaker information
for brochure.   126

❏ Communicate with speaker and musicians.   126

❏ Host the speaker or ask the pastor's wife to host
the speaker during lunch.   126

❏ Confirm sound, lighting, details.   126

❏ Find fabulous door prize; design door prize form.   125

❏ Invite the pastor's wife to host or give the welcome at the luncheon.   126

❏ Plan a minute-by-minute schedule for program personalities.   126

❏ Keep the program on schedule.   126

❏ Prepare a notebook of ideas for future luncheons.   127

❏ Communicate often with women's ministry and promotions
coordinators.   126

❏ Designate leaders for food, decor, tickets, prayer, hostesses, etc.   125

❏ Food planner sets menu, assures food preparation and service.   126

❏ Tickets coordinator prints tickets and plans seating and ticket sales.   125

❏ Hostess recruits a hostess for each table, trains hostesses, and meets with hostesses for prayer before luncheon.   124

❏ Mini-special leader plans and oversees strict ten-minute highlight.   126

❏ Greeters may be the responsibility of the women's ministry hospitality coordinator.   128

❏ Decor leader plans and prepares decorations for entry,
table, and podium.   127

APPENDIX 3

Checklist for Hospitality Coordinator

		Page
❑	Recruit greeters.	65
❑	Recruit women for registration desk.	64
❑	Plan registration desk setup, snack setup.	64
❑	Prepare signup list for snacks.	73
❑	Make a plan for a women's ministry roster or directory.	70
❑	Prepare weekly snack reminder cards or phone plan.	73
❑	Design registration form for women's ministry.	69
❑	Research name tags; order after kickoff/before day one.	70
❑	Assign snack setup volunteer for decor and drink preparation.	73
❑	Plan expeditious sign-in process for kickoff and weekly meetings.	60
❑	Plan coffee break room setup.	73
❑	Make plans for ordering name tags on kickoff afternoon.	70

Checklist for Ministry Teams Coordinator

	Page
❏ Meet with women's ministry coordinator and pastor or staff liaison for input about needed ministry teams.	88
❏ Evaluate potential ministry teams by parameters.	80
❏ Prayerfully research and select this year's ministry teams.	88
❏ Recruit a leader for each ministry team.	89
❏ Ministry team leaders develop their individual plans.	91
❏ Obtain ministry team descriptions for brochure.	89
❏ Assist ministry team leaders with resources and encouragement.	90
❏ Assure ministry team leaders are well prepared.	30
❏ Begin a notebook of potential ministry teams and leaders.	83
❏ Prepare directional signs for ministry team send-off sites.	90
❏ Assist planning presentation of ministry teams for kickoff event.	60
❏ Plan one meeting of all ministry team leaders.	90
❏ Take part in each ministry team occasionally.	90

❏ Take photos of ministry teams in action.   90
❏ Plan a social gathering for ministry team leaders (tea or lunch).   90

APPENDIX 5

Checklist for Fellowship Class Coordinator

                                                                          Page

❏ Plan a year's curriculum of Bible, missions, crafts, and
   interest classes.   98

❏ Assure variety of classes each semester.   99

❏ Recruit qualified teachers for each class.   101

❏ Approve and order Bible study and missions materials.   102

❏ Assist class leaders with kickoff presentation preparation.   61

❏ Assist and encourage class leaders as needed.   31

❏ Provide class descriptions for brochure.   139

❏ Make room assignments for fellowship classes.   104

❏ Prepare directional signs or door signs for classes.   98

❏ Assist fellowship class teachers with preparation if needed.   99

❏ Provide supply lists or study materials for purchase at kickoff.   60

❏ Plan visible location for mission education table near registration.   107

APPENDIX 6

Checklist for Promotion Coordinator

❏ Recruit artistic, creative women to assist with publicity. 136

❏ Select font, color, theme, etc., to use this year. 139

❏ If no logo exists, design a women's ministry logo. 139

❏ Make a written one-year publicity plan. 135

❏ Design and print a quality brochure with semester or year schedule. 139

❏ Create an outside promotion plan (for those outside the church): 144

    ❏ Exterior church sign

    ❏ Local newspaper community events

    ❏ Local newspaper story or photo

    ❏ Business cards for members to invite friends

    ❏ T-shirts

    ❏ E-invitation sent to members to forward to friends

    ❏ Extra handouts for members to give friends

    ❏ Mass mail-out to community or target group

❏ Create inside promotion items (for women in church): 139

    ❏ Bulletin announcements (reworded weekly)

- ❏ Church newsletter articles
- ❏ Church Web site
- ❏ Phone tree, occasional
- ❏ New member packets
- ❏ Visitor packets
- ❏ Posters and visuals in church building
- ❏ Flyers
- ❏ Handouts
- ❏ Pulpit promotion
- ❏ Sunday school ambassadors
- ❏ Telephone guests from last Sunday
- ❏ Display racks
- ❏ Bulletin insert (one per year)
- ❏ Personal invitation plan

Did Women of the Bible LIGHT?

Is there a biblical basis for women's involvement in hands-on ministry? Absolutely! Throughout God's Word, commands are given and illustrations shared of women going, helping, and touching others in God's name.

Jesus Christ himself elevated the position of women through His words and His actions. He said, "You are all sons of God through faith in Christ Jesus. For as many of you as have been baptized into Christ have put on Christ. There is no Jew or Greek, slave or free, male or female; for you are all one in Christ Jesus" (Gal. 3:26–28).

All Christians are commanded to use their spiritual gifts through the church. "Now there are different gifts, but the same Spirit. There are different ministries, but the same Lord. And there are different activities, but the same God is active in everyone and everything" (1 Cor. 12:4–6).

We are admonished as Christians to be faithful in the use of our gifts to his service. "Based on the gift they have received, everyone should use it to serve others, as good managers of the varied grace of God" (1 Pet. 4:10).

Examples of Biblical Women Ministering

Numerous examples are given of women who ministered in God's name. The Old Testament tells of Abishag (1 Kings 1:3–4) who cared for King David when he was ill. The widow of Zarapath (1 Kings 17) shared her meager food and water with a stranger, and the maid of Naaman's wife (2 Kings 5) fearlessly shared her faith with her master. The Proverbs 31 woman opened her arms to the poor and extended her hands to the needy.

The New Testament boasts of a disciple named Dorcas who was always doing good and helping the poor (Acts 9:36). All the widows wept when she died and showed Peter the robes and clothes she had made. Mary of Bethany was an effective evangelist, and many who came to visit her believed in Jesus (John 11:45; 12:9–11). Anna, an elderly widow, went out to proclaim good tidings (Luke 2:36–38). Lydia won her servants to Christ and showed her love in gracious hospitality. Priscilla labored together with her husband in the service of the church. Philip's daughters prophesied about Christ (Acts 21:8–9). Paul wrote of his remembrance of Timothy's sincere faith, which first lived in Timothy's grandmother, Lois, and his mother, Eunice (1 Tim. 1:5). In Paul's letter to the Romans, he sent greetings to Tryphena, Tryphosa, Persis, and Mary, who "worked very hard in the Lord" (Rom. 16:12). He also commended Phoebe, "a servant of the church in Cenchreae . . . for . . . she has been a benefactor of many—and of me also" (Rom. 16:1–2).

In a discussion about older widows in the church, Paul stated, "No widow should be placed on the official support list unless she . . . is well known for good works—that is, if she has brought up children, shown hospitality, washed the saints' feet, helped the afflicted, and devoted herself to every good work" (1 Tim. 5:9–10). This suggests that a woman's reputation for doing good works is a desirable trait. Scripture also teaches that a woman's beauty should not come from outward adornment but should be an inner beauty.

A Command to Minister

Scripture teaches that Christians should be known for their good deeds. A stirring command is given for Christians to show their faith in Christ by their works, concluding with the statement that "faith without works is dead" (James 2:14–26). Scripture teaches that every good tree bears good fruit (Matt. 7:17), and states that Christians will be recognized by their fruit (Matt. 7:16).

Consider this challenge: "We must not get tired of doing good, for we will reap at the proper time if we don't give up. Therefore, as we have opportunity, we must work for the good of all, especially for those who belong to the household of faith" (Gal. 6:9–10). Christians are to "show family affection to one another with brotherly love. Outdo one another in showing honor. Do not lack diligence; be fervent in spirit; serve the Lord. Rejoice in hope; be patient in affliction; be persistent in prayer. Share with the saints in their needs; pursue hospitality" (Rom. 12:10–13). Still another Scripture encourages us to live a life that shows our good deeds. "Conduct yourselves honorably among the Gentiles, so that in a case where they speak against you as those who do evil, they may, by observing your good works, glorify God in a day of visitation" (1 Pet. 2:12).

Christians are instructed to live a life of doing good to others, "to do good, to be rich in good works, to be generous, willing to share" (1 Tim. 6:18).

This sampling of Scripture clearly demonstrates that God expects his followers to be about the business of ministering to others in His name.

Our model women's ministry, LIGHT, used Matthew 25:34–40 (see page 80) to evaluate potential ministry teams, along with a requirement that they be done in Jesus' name (Col. 3:17). His Great Commission to His disciples demands that we go in Jesus' name (Matt. 28:19–20).

Yes, women of the Bible did practice ministry to others. They were ladies intentionally going, helping, and touching. LIGHT your world.

Resources

A great women's ministry leader reads everything on the topic! Challenge every leader to become an expert on her area of ministry. Successful church women's ministry leaders provided this sampling of their favorites:

Books

Adams, Chris. *Women Reaching Women: Beginning and Building a Growing Women's Ministry*. Nashville: LifeWay Press, 2005.

Adams, Chris. *Transformed Lives*. Nashville: LifeWay Press, 2000.

Briscoe, Jill, Laurie Katz McIntyre, and Beth Seversen. *Designing Effective Women's Ministries*. Grand Rapids: Zondervan, 1995.

Davis, Diana. *Fresh Ideas: 1000 Ways to Grow a Thriving and Energetic Church*. Nashville: B&H Publishing Group, 2007.

Duncan, J. Ligon and Susan Hunt. *Women's Ministry in the Local Church*. Wheaton: Crossway, 2006.

Focus on the Family Women's Ministry Guide. Gospel Light, 2005.

Group Compilation. *Women's Ministry in the 21st Century*. Loveland, Colo.: Group Publishing, 2004.

Jaynes, Sharon. *Building an Effective Women's Ministry*. Eugene: Harvest House, 2005.

Kraft, Vickie and Gwynne Johnson. *Women Mentoring Women: Ways to Start, Maintain, and Expand a Biblical Women's Ministry*. Chicago: Moody, 2003.

Martin, Jaye. *HeartCall*, Women's Evangelism materials (www.namb.net).

North American Mission Board. *The Net* outreach materials and *His Heart Our Hands* community evangelism materials (www.namb.net).

Porter, Carol. *The Women's Ministry Handbook*. Wheaton, Ill.: Victor, 1992.

Robinson, Ella. *I Can Do That Too! More Ways to be on Mission*. Birmingham: Women's Missionary Union, 2006.

Schaller, Lyle E. *44 Ways to Revitalize the Women's Organization*. Nashville: Abingdon Press, 1990.

Professional Assistance

Take a seminary class on women's ministry (see http.//sbc.net/aboutus/sem.asp).

Contact your denomination's state or local women's ministry/missions department for consultation and additional resources (see www.sbc.net/stateconvassoc.asp).

Web Sites

Find thousands of ideas and resources at these sites.

www.lifeway.com/women	Women's ministry conferencess, consultations, ideas
www.wmu.com	Women on Mission, missionaries, Bible studies
www.namb.net/women	Evangelism materials, North American Missions
www.namb.net	North American missions, community ministry idea
www.imb.org	Foreign mission ideas, facts, maps, videos, resources
www.womenonmission.com	Women on Mission programs, projects, resources
www.lifeway.com	Bible studies, topical books and resources

Magazines

On Mission	*The Commission*
Missions Mosaic	*Deacon Magazine*
To the Ends of the Earth	

**Sample of Logo
(Used by permission)**

Logo designed by Dixie Scogin.
Used by permission.

Jesus Loves Through Me

Lyrics by: Randy Lind

Music by: Randy Lind

I'LL LET MY LIGHT SHINE____ EV-RY WHERE____ I GO. I'LL LET MY

LIGHT SHINE____ SO ALL THE WORLD WILL KNOW. I'LL LET MY LIGHT SHINE____ SO

ALL THE WORLD WILL SEE THAT JE-SUS LOVES THEM,____ JE-SUS LOVES THEM.____

JE - SUS LOVES____ THROUGH ME.

Used by permission. May be
enlarged and photocopied.

About the Author

Diana Davis is a women's ministry consultant for the State Convention of Baptists in Indiana. She is also a popular speaker for women's conferences and retreats and seminars for pastors' and deacons' wives.

Her extensive experience in organizing and leading the women's ministry in her church resulted in major success, both in enrollment and impact on church growth. She uses strategic planning methods to combine discipleship, ministry teams and missions.

Diana and her husband served as pastor and wife in Texas churches for more than three decades before moving to Indiana, where he serves as the Baptist state convention's executive director.

She writes a regular column for *Let's Worship* magazine and *Deacon Magazine*. Her "Fresh Ideas" articles are regularly featured in the *Indiana Baptist Monthly* and numerous other state and national Baptist publications. Her articles have been featured on LifeWay's Pastors Today e-Newsletter and Rick Warren's Pastors.com.

When Diana is not writing or traveling, she relishes a good book on her condo rooftop, strolls around downtown Indy, and spending time with family and friends. Her three adult children live in Texas, Ohio, and England.

Diana's first B&H book *Fresh Ideas: 1000 Ways to Grow a Thriving and Energetic Church* was released in 2007. Her upcoming book for deacon wives is scheduled to release in 2009.

E-mail the author at Jesuslivesindiana@gmail.com or visit her Web site at www.keeponshining.com.